Henry Jr

THE FORGOTTEN MAJOR

(in the siege of Imphal)

THE FORGOTTEN MAJOR

(in the siege of Imphal)

DAVID ATKINS

THE TOAT PRESS
PULBOROUGH, WEST SUSSEX

First published in 1989 by The Toat Press,
Tullens Toat, Pulborough, West Sussex RH20 1DA

© 1989 David Atkins

All rights reserved. No part of this publication may be reproduced, stored in a retrieval system or transmitted in any form or by any means, electronic, mechanical, photocopying, recording or otherwise, without the prior permission of the publisher.

British Library Cataloguing in Publication Data

Atkins, David, 1916
   The forgotten major : in the siege of Imphal.
   1. World War 2. Burma campaign. Army operations by India. — Army
   I. Title
   940.54'25

ISBN 0-9511063-1-7

Typeset by Pauline Newton, Chichester, West Sussex
Printed in the United Kingdom by Villiers Publications Ltd, 26a Shepherds Hill, London N6 5AH

CONTENTS

Chapter		Page
	Introduction	1
1	Revival	3
2	The Tiddim Track	12
3	The Vegetable Fraud	23
4	The Monsoon	32
5	Grinding Discipline	42
6	Cobras	51
7	A Girl and a Mutiny	64
8	Calm before the Storm	71
9	Start of the Battle	79
10	The Slogging Match	88
11	The Enemy Breaks	102
12	Mohammedan versus Hindu	112
13	End of the War in Europe	119
14	Forgotten and Left Behind	126
15	The Atom Bomb and Peace	132
	Appendix I	141
	Appendix II	142
	Appendix III	143

LIST OF PLATES
Between pages 82 and 83

The author, Bill Greenbury and Bruce Rust. Poona 1940
Letter sent on Christmas Day 1942
Pioneers on the Tiddim Track 1943
Max Gray on the Tiddim Track 1943
A Kuki village
Elephants coming up river at Tiphaimukh with grain barges
The Imphal Plain March 1944
The Imphal 'Keep', with airfield and 4 Corps Headquarters
Imphal Plain looking south from Bishenpur
Tamu road
George Dorrington on the Silchar Track
Major at last. Tim Eaton with the Dutch girls
Author in point-to-point at Delhi 1942
Senior staff
George Dorrington, Margaret Eaton, Paula Atkins, the author

LIST OF MAPS
(pages xi–xiii)

Map of India
Japanese attack 10th to 31st March 1944
Limit of Japanese advance, end of May 1944

ACKNOWLEDGEMENTS

Most of this book is based on my own memories supported by my letters to my father and from the personal reminiscences of people I knew in Imphal. I have also used information from the many letters I received after the publication of *The Reluctant Major*.

As the book progressed however I found myself relying a great deal for verification of facts and dates upon *Burma, The Longest War* by Louis Allen (published by J.M. Dent and Sons Ltd). This book also considerably increased my knowledge of the movements and strategy of the Japanese forces. I acknowledge with gratitude my debt to Louis Allen.

The other books from which I have quoted are *Imphal* by Sir George Evans and Anthony Brett-James (published by Macmillan and Co. Ltd), *The Air Battle of Imphal* by Norman Franks (published by William Kimber) and *Defeat Into Victory* by Field-Marshal The Viscount Slim. The following books by authors I either know or have known have been helpful: *A Sapper in the Forgotten Army* by John Henslow, *Naga Path* by Ursula Bower, *Then a Soldier* by Peter Collister, and *Elephant Bill* by J.H. Williams.

Many people have been generous with their personal accounts and their letters. In particular I owe a debt to my brother Sinclair Atkins, who was present throughout the siege, to Pat Tidy who was the adjutant on the Tiddim Track, to George Dorrington, Gordon Rolfe and Gordon Sheldon, all of whom served with me, to Ben Bazeley who has written an interesting account of the events in the area, and to Phillip Malins, a mule expert. The following, among others, have given me information on the siege: Bruce Rust, Peter Longmore, Brian Godfrey, Bill Reynolds, Cecil Bendall, Bob Elliott, Ian Keith, Raj Fowler, Marian Carswell, Martha Davies, Alec Binnie, Kenneth Capel-Cure, Robert Glennie, Henry Birtwistle, L.F. Richards, C.R. Jenkinson, Norman Bennett and Max Gray.

Thanks also to Jon Wynne-Tyson for background support, to Edward Enfield and Norman Cowling who read and advised on the early drafts, and to my son John who drew the maps. Finally, to my wife Paula who has not only with good humour and affection put up with piles of papers and letters spread about the house but has also been a gentle and excellent critic whose advice I have usually taken.

FOREWORD
by
The Rt Hon. Viscount Slim OBE, DL

Never before has an Army had to fight and win a war against such a tough, tenacious, vicious and courageous foe as the Jap; this mostly within tortuous, steep and rugged jungle terrain which demanded more than average hand-to-hand combat. That was challenging enough, but add to this the appalling, tenuous and almost non-existent lines of its communication that must be rapidly built to ensure the survival and reinforcement of its corps and divisions in order to enable the Army to battle and conquer, then a daunting task emerges. Never mind the enemy, the stage is not set without including the devastating effects of climate and monsoon, allied with the killer diseases of malaria, dysentery and scrub typhus. There were in this Army soldiers of many races and religions who had already fought in Burma in the largest retreat in British history, been beaten by the Jap, and forced to stare at the stark realities of defeat. There was much to be done to guarantee victory.

In its early days, such was the lot of the Fourteenth Army in Assam and Burma.

The Forgotten Army was not given the tools for the job. The Burma Campaign was low, if not at the bottom of, national wartime priorities. The Army to win had to help itself and it did so with a vengeance. Thus improvisation became the norm at every level. Nowhere was self-help, local invention and initiative more evident than from those who worked on the lines of communication in the forward and rear echelons.

David Atkins shows in this book and *The Reluctant Major*, though underplaying crises in a laid-back British style, the harsh dangers and problems of those who toiled tirelessly to keep the

Fourteenth Army fighting. His was, like so many in Burma, an independent, isolated and lonely command. Not easy when essentials are non-existent, information lacking and any immediate support seldom available. A tough situation for any of field rank and the Author shows clearly that initiative, leadership and sensible discipline are not just the prerogative of the frontline warrior. Like many of us with the experience of several generations of the Indian Continent, David Atkins has affection for its people and soldiers, with the sense of humour that all must have to survive in action.

My father always said, "Victory in Burma came, not from the work of any one man, or even a few men, but from the sum of many men's efforts." He would not have minded the Author getting the rum ration increased to the advantage of the Army! He was proud of Officers like David Atkins, his junior Officers, NCOs and the soldiers of 309 Company who kept the Army going forward. The Fourteenth Army had men of many nationalities who in adversity produced the leadership, spirit and the guts to win. Those of us who know do not forget.

SLIM
House of Lords
September 1988

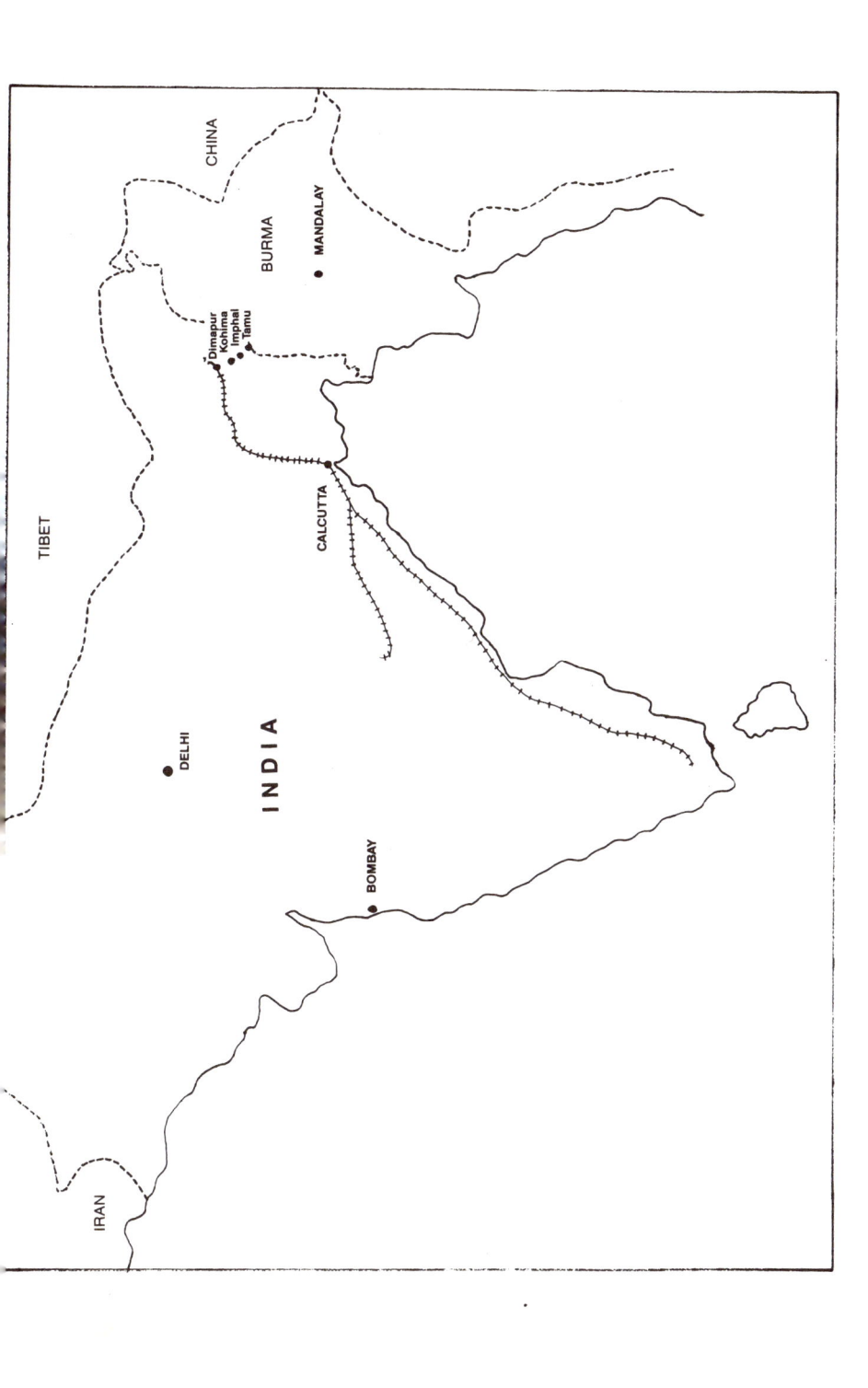

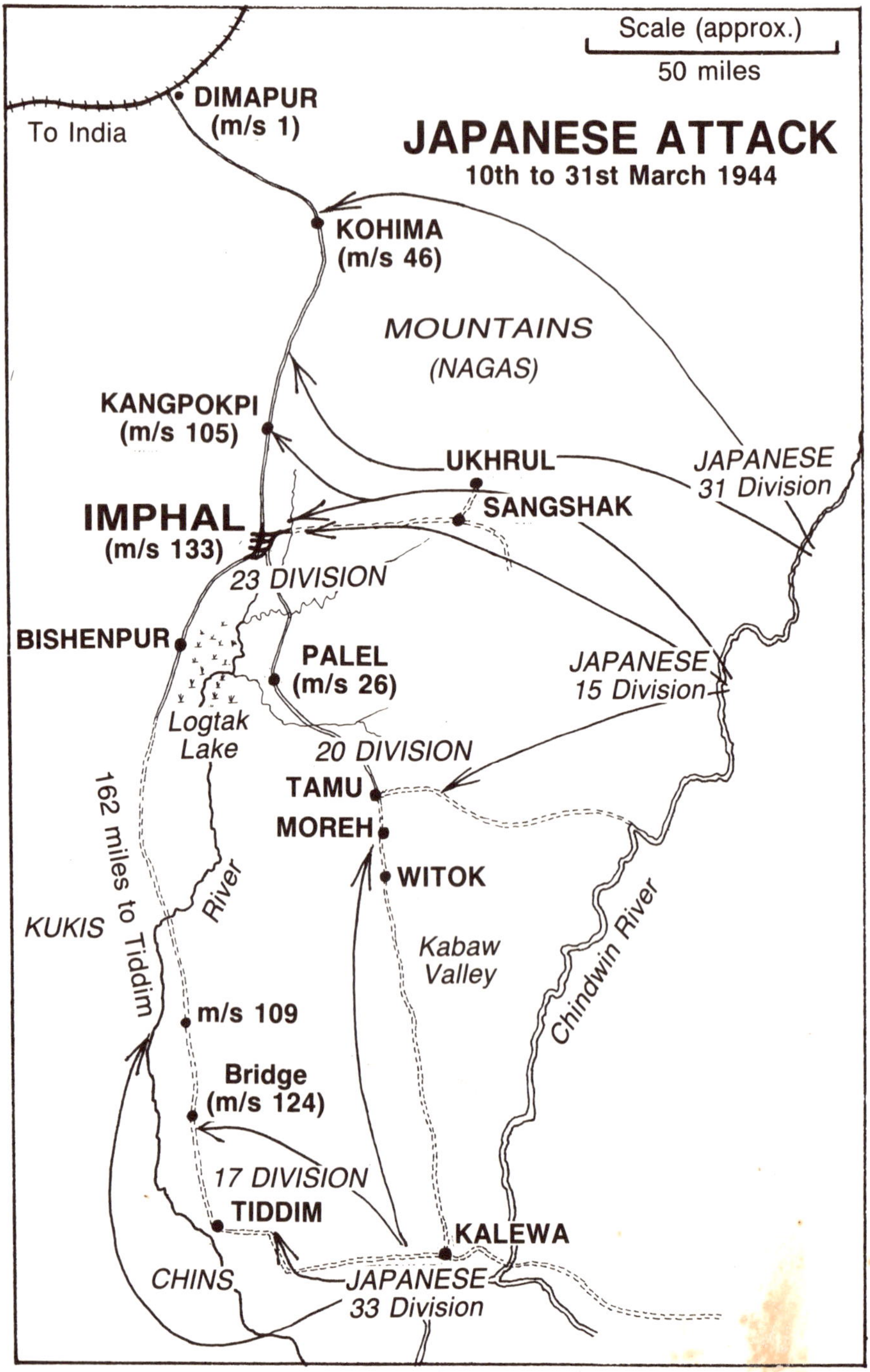

Scale (approx.)
50 miles
JAPANESE ATTACK
10th to 31st March 1944
To India
DIMAPUR
(m/s 1)
KOHIMA
(m/s 46)
MOUNTAINS
(NAGAS)
KANGPOKPI
(m/s 105)
UKHRUL
SANGSHAK
JAPANESE
31 Division
IMPHAL
(m/s 133)
23 DIVISION
BISHENPUR
PALEL
(m/s 26)
JAPANESE
15 Division
Logtak
Lake
20 DIVISION
TAMU
MOREH
WITOK
162 miles to Tiddim
River
KUKIS
Kabaw
Valley
Chindwin River
m/s 109
Bridge
(m/s 124)
17 DIVISION
TIDDIM
KALEWA
CHINS
JAPANESE
33 Division

LIMIT OF JAPANESE ADVANCE
End of May 1944

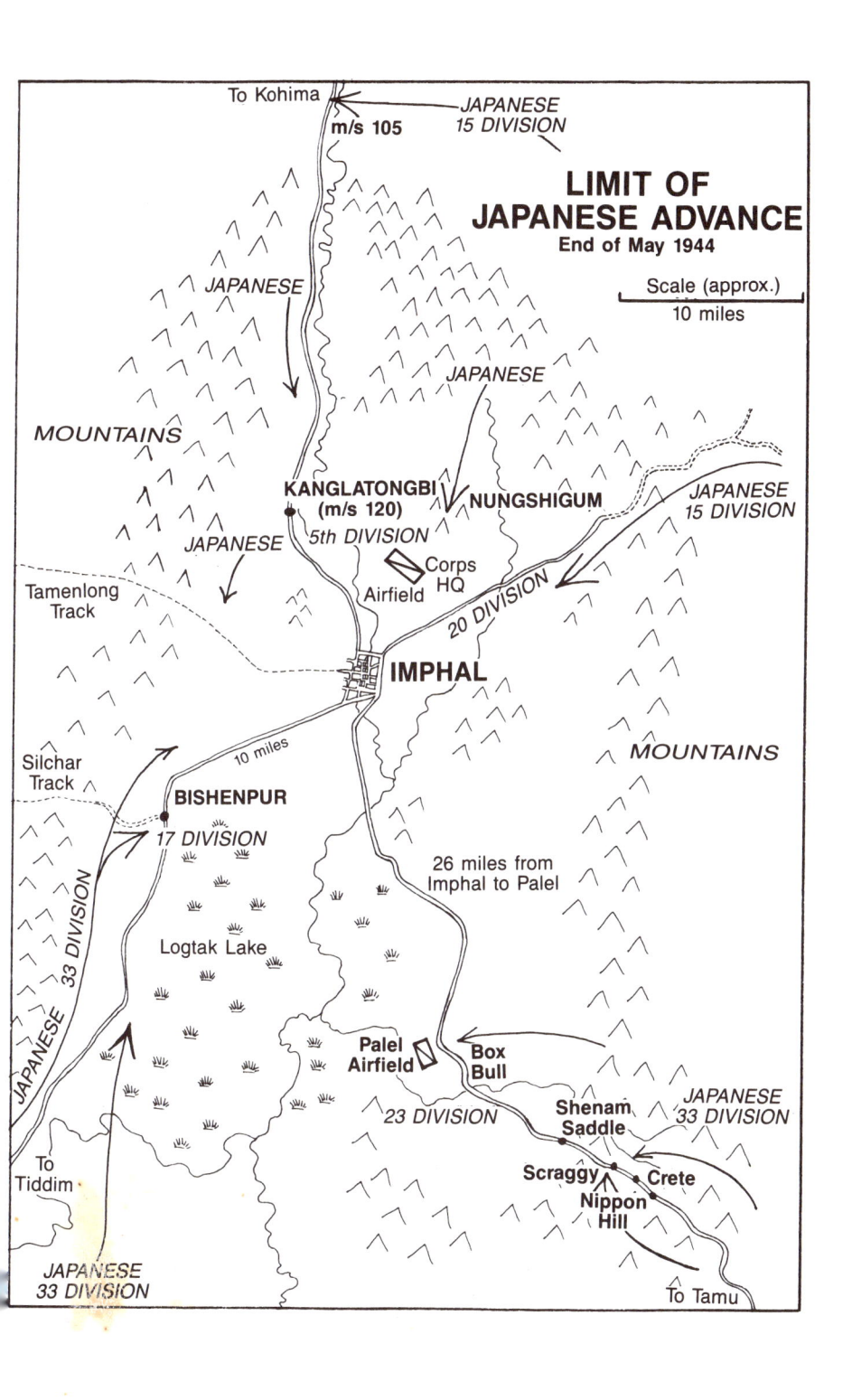

Map showing the Imphal battlefield at the end of May 1944.

Key locations and features:
- To Kohima / m/s 105
- JAPANESE 15 DIVISION
- MOUNTAINS
- KANGLATONGBI (m/s 120) — 5th DIVISION
- NUNGSHIGUM
- Corps HQ / Airfield
- 20 DIVISION
- Tamenlong Track
- IMPHAL
- Silchar Track
- BISHENPUR — 17 DIVISION
- 10 miles
- Logtak Lake
- 26 miles from Imphal to Palel
- JAPANESE 33 DIVISION
- To Tiddim
- Palel Airfield
- Box Bull
- 23 DIVISION
- Shenam Saddle
- Scraggy • Crete
- Nippon Hill
- JAPANESE 33 DIVISION
- To Tamu

Scale (approx.) 10 miles

INTRODUCTION

This book is a sequel to *The Reluctant Major* of which an outline is perhaps necessary.

I did not wish to be promoted to Major. I did not want to leave the exciting life of a young officer in Delhi but I was kicked out and upstairs.

As a staff officer I had made two big mistakes. I had slipped a decimal point in a calculation and as a result orders went out for rum for 20,000,000 soldiers instead of 2,000,000. I had also, with the North African campaign in mind, sent all the spare flour in Northern India to be stored in Karachi on the West Coast when suddenly it was needed in the East for the Japanese War. I was sacked, but as the army was desperate for officers who understood India and as I had passed the Urdu exam, I was promoted at once to Major and went off to raise a Transport Company.

In April 1942 I reached Jhansi and was sent some 450 young sepoys recruited from villages all over Southern India. They spoke no English or Urdu and had six different languages of their own but none in common. My officers, both English and Indian, were all as untrained as I was.

I was told to get the Company ready for active service in three months. We taught ourselves how to command, our men how to drive and obey orders, and indeed we made soldiers of them and of ourselves.

By August 1942 we were on the Burma front, driving heavy lorries up mountainous dirt roads in monsoon rain. Every time we ferried supplies the 120 miles to the front we lost 5% of our lorries over the edge. This we could have coped with, but then disaster struck.

With no anti-malaria medicine at all, my men went down with fever. By the end of September 1942 we were down to six fit men and my lorries were strewn deserted over 120 miles of road and cliff. Many of my men had vanished, some died on the roadside or in the unmanned and useless hospitals. The casualty rate for malaria in 1942 was 600% (*really* six hundred per cent!) a year and on the Imphal front there was then only one man who escaped malaria and that by chance was me. Because of this in the end I was the officer with the longest continuous service in that area.

By November 1942 malaria had wrought such havoc with the army that the ten transport companies with 1200 vehicles between them could together hardly muster enough men to put 120 lorries on the road each day. Supplies to the front failed and the fighting troops were withdrawn behind us back to India.

A complete reorganisation took place (it failed) and in the course of this we were sent forward. We were then the Transport Company closest to the Japanese and with no infantry in front of us. At this point in January 1943 this book begins. It concerns the long campaign around Imphal.

This town, which lies in the centre of the lovely plain of Manipur State, is surrounded by range after range of wild mountains. Three thousand feet up and with a good climate, the plain was connected to India only by a 130-mile single track road and to Burma by two footpaths. By geographical chance it was the key point for any attack on India and also for any advance into Burma.

Chapter 1

REVIVAL

At the end of 1942 the British in India were at the end of their tether. All their trained troops were in the Middle East or had been lost in Singapore and Burma. The will to fight was lacking as both British and Indian soldiers thought the Japanese unbeatable. There was not a trained Division in reserve anywhere and plans were being made back in Calcutta to blow all the road and railway bridges leading to central India.

If, with its internal security already under pressure from a militant Congress, India had collapsed as had Malaya and Singapore, the Japanese dream of linking up across Persia with the triumphant German forces near the Black Sea could have become a reality.

This is the story of how the Indian Army, which for a brief time on the Burma front had been almost incapable of fighting, recovered to inflict on the enemy their greatest land defeat of the war.

* * * * *

Perhaps the strengthening in morale began on the Tiddim Track. The idea of changing a 3-foot wide mountain path, which ran for 150 miles across some of the wildest mountains in the world, into a motor road, was thought up in Delhi. It was conceived by Wavell and Slim who, smarting from their defeats, nevertheless still believed in their troops.

Through that wall of mountain which ran for 750 miles along the frontier between us and the enemy, there were only three gaps and this gave the opposing armies contact on fronts which in total were less than 40 miles wide. The Tiddim Track opened up a fourth area of contact and gave us a chance, never used, of cutting the line of supply of Japanese troops further north.

It was an idea which had strange results. Everyone working and fighting on the Tiddim Track loved the road and when we had built it, the army that used it best was the Japanese. By a quirk of war, because they used it so well, they were drawn down it to a terrible end.

It was a strange life on the Track: ten thousand men, none of them fighting soldiers, spread out on both sides of the narrow mountainous road which finally led by a mule track to Tiddim. Away from the road itself there were only mountains and jungle. Beyond Tiddim the line was held by 'V' Force, which consisted of a few British officers with levies from the Hill Tribes. The infantry and the Divisions were far behind us and not even a bren gun stood between us and the Japanese. No one however had the energy to fight and the Japanese and Indian armies had drawn apart exhausted and sick.

Our Company, having failed to carry out its job on the Dimapur–Imphal road, now found itself in December '42, stranded like a beached whale at Milestone 32. I knew this was my last chance, I had to get the Company working properly or I would be out on my ear.

About the middle of January 1943, there began a remarkable turn-around. Malaria had stopped because the cold weather had killed the mosquitoes; dysentery for the time being seemed on the wane and up the Tiddim Track reinforcements came pouring.

I was entitled to six officers but by the end of January I had eight. Also to my great pleasure there arrived a qualified European REME Warrant Officer with the odd rank of Sub-Conductor. Snowden was an excellent and energetic man and fitted in at once. Shortly afterwards, to cap it all, two good British REME Sergeants, Goodbury and Minnit, also arrived.

They were very different characters. Sergeant Minnit was quiet and withdrawn and wrote a letter home every day of his life. Sergeant Goodbury had run a fish and chip shop in the East End of London and looked like it. He was a firm disciplinarian, tough as old boots, but oddly enough could not hold his drink.

All the workshop staff found Sergeant Goodbury's English amusing. For the first time for months they had to wear hats, although only on parade first thing. "Get your bloody titfer", (tit-for-tat — hat) became a workshop joke. Soon all of them were talking rhyming slang; it was an 'in' thing with them. The morale of the workshop rose as they ceased to think of themselves as attachments to our vehicle platoons, but as 'the workshop' which alone could understand that a star (star spangled banner) was a spanner.

Everyone on the Tiddim Track began to clean up their uniforms and equipment, to catch up with their records, and even to mount guards. The mounting of guards, to the dismay of some Regulars, had been the first thing to go when the companies collapsed. We still however continued to use shallow latrines as Colonel Towers, who commanded the Track, had ordered us not to dig deep ones. The road was being built so fast that we had all moved on by the time the flies hatched out in the latrines.

Our company worked regular hours, was well fed, had clean streams in which to bathe, firewood for the taking, and flowers including roses and lilies for the picking. Now the men when washed could put on clean clothes and some would, to our surprise, put flowers behind their ears. The mess orderly turned out to be a good flower arranger and with a mixture of green leaves and white flowers with a splash of red, he gave the officers' mess a new look. My will to survive strengthened as, for the first time for months, things were going right.

One of our problems during that winter was keeping the men warm. The white frosts in the morning amazed them. They came from a soft climate near the equator, where the temperature is always between 80–100°F. If you gave them extra blankets, they lay on them, and we had the ridiculous necessity of giving lectures on how to keep warm in bed and on the use of underclothes and pullovers.

The freezing mornings made the men more lax in the cleaning of cooking pots in the streams. On one occasion when I was pitching into Koshy, the officer concerned, he disarmed me with his erudition:

"Is it not much like Shakespeare, sahib," he said, "when greasy Joan doth keel the pot? See how we also keel the pots with sticks and sand."

"Jemadar sahib," I replied, "when next you re-enact Shakespeare's words, please see the pots are properly keeled, bilkul (absolutely) clean, just as greasy Joan would have keeled them." I never ceased being amazed that so many of my senior staff knew Shakespeare's works intimately.

At 'lights out' a mosquito patrol toured the tents and bashas. Any man who had not put up a net lost a month's pay at my next orderly room, and anyone who slept with an arm or leg against a mosquito net was hit with a light cane. After a time, the men lay straight in the centre of their nets; our mosquito discipline had begun to bite!

Although our work was regular and ordered, Towers drove us ahead without rest days even on Sundays; it was extraordinary that such a low-ranking officer (he was only a Lieutenant-Colonel) should have commanded so many men. He signed no papers himself but left all his administration to his adjutant Pat Tidy. Pat was a gnome-like figure, who looked odd because he had shaved his head. He was recognised from afar because he wore a Gurkha hat, a hat of which he was very fond and which he tells me was eventually siezed from him by an American officer on VJ night in Piccadilly. Towers had complete command of every unit on the road. It all worked marvellously and above all I found myself working for a man I admired.

Engineers are reputed to be mad, methodist or married, and Tidy perhaps came in the mad catgory. He had brought his civilian bearer, a Mohammedan, right up into the war area — unauthorised of course — and this man stood behind his chair in spotless white — white clothes broke the camouflage regulations — and wore around his waist a broad cummerbund in the red and blue colours of the Royal Engineers with a similar flash of colour on his pugri. Tidy's job just before he came up the Track was to plan for the blowing up of all the bridges in Calcutta on the arrival of the Japanese. That makes one realise how close we were to panic and defeat in late 1942.

We had no visits from Brigadiers or Generals for those few months; most of them were still back in Jorhat, three hundred miles away, where 14th Army was trying to regroup. In July 1942 Wavell had not had a single division left in India fit to fight but now the army was recovering.

Of my platoons three were spread up and down the track and we were kept very busy, moving units forward and carrying hardcore and supplies of all sorts. I had only to drive forty miles to see them all.

By February the road was reaching forward fast and a Jeep Transport Company arrived straight from the plains of India. It was commanded by 'Jeepo' Reid. It worked closely with Tim Eaton, the officer commanding my forward platoon. 'Jeepo', a stout officer, smoked cigars all the time. On one occasion his jeep overturned and he was pinned down. The lighted cigar was still in his hand when he smelt petrol dripping onto his body. He could hardly move his arm but managed to get the cigar up to his mouth and put the lighted end in. It took two or three minutes to put out the cigar with his tongue. When rescued Jeepo could not eat properly for several weeks.

Just before we had received orders to move up to the Burma front, my excellent captain had collapsed with heat stroke. I had promoted my most senior officer Johnson who had been with me only a short time. It had been a mistake; from the first we did not get on well and this was exacerbated by the fact that he despised Indians as a race, while I who had known them all my life, saw them as individuals and liked most of them.

We were soon on bad terms and I sent him with the fourth platoon to Palel on the Tamu Road, seventy miles away from me. With constant attacks of malaria, he had gone a little mad. He was naturally a bully and, as he became more aware that his platoon disliked him, his discipline grew very odd: he developed a habit, which I did not hear about until later, of threatening with his pistol anyone who was slow or stupid in carrying out orders.

It is necessary to explain the rank of Viceroy Commissioned Officer. A King's Commissioned Officer might be British or Indian and could serve in any of the armies, British, Dominion or Indian. A VCO could only serve in the Indian army, but could be promoted to KCO. The Indian Army contained half the number of KCOs as the British Army and this deficiency was made up by VCOs. VCOs were entitled to officer privileges, e.g. a soldier servant.

The Indian Army relied for the detailed knowledge of special problems, which is so necessary in a good unit, on a feedback of information through VCOs to KCOs. As our adjutant Subahdar Bhagwan Das was a Punjabi Hindu and Johnson's VCO was an inexperienced Mahratta who spoke none of the men's languages, the flow of intelligence from his platoon up to me was nonexistent. The position went rapidly from bad to worse. I did not pay them enough visits, and as I was not in direct touch with his Engineer units, I had no idea how dissatisfied they were with his platoon's work. This was all to break on me later.

Tim Eaton was still forward and attached to Colonel Towers' personal mess. He was very haggard and on edge, and was still feeling the death of his VCO who had been killed a few weeks earlier. His special delight was in disaster. He would come down and stay with me, looking like a rather small and moulting eagle, and over a drink of rum he would start.

"You realise, David, that the monsoon is expected early this year and the road will be washed away."

"Tim," I replied, "you know the Engineers have put in a hell of a lot of large culverts."

"That won't help when each little stream rises thirty feet in a night."

With two hundred inches of rain a year falling in four months he was right in expecting flash floods. Above the small bridges on the Track one could see the debris from old storms caught twenty feet up in the trees. The Engineers had built the bridges to cope with the normal flow only and their intention was to let the floods flow over the roads.

Tim, having got me worried, vanished into the mess to count the rum bottles and consult with the mess orderly.

"It's ten days until the next rum issue," he said emerging, "and as you have eight gallons, I suggest I take up a few with me just to look after them for you."

Pooh Bear counting honey jars and Tim Eaton counting rum bottles had a lot in common.

Up till then we had had no fighting troops in front of us but at the end of March 1943, 17 Division with its sign of a black cat with its tail up went through us and up the Track to Tiddim. From the end of our motor road, jeeps were operating but from Milestone 109 the Division was supplied only by mule trains which trekked up the 'Chocolate Staircase'. This was a series of hairpin bends rising 3000 feet up from the valley and was built by the fighting troops of 17 Division.

Behind Tim's platoon back along the road, we had two new officers who got on well together but had entirely different life styles. Drurie-Brewer was an amiable plump thirty-five-year-old, who had worked in India with Imperial Chemicals and was used to a high standard of living. He spoke Urdu and looked like a contented clergyman. When one stayed with him the bathwater was hot, there was a large dry towel, the drink was cooled in a nearby stream, and one sat down to a three-course dinner, served on china plates.

On the other hand, to stay with Paddy Hargreaves, which I rarely did after my first visit, was very different. He lived hard, took little notice of what he ate, and dinner might come up from the men's cookhouse on enamel plates.

Both these officer's platoons were well run and the two of them had developed an amiable rivalry in which there was no snide undercurrent.

"I am worried about Drurie-Brewer," Hargreaves would say. "I had dinner with him last night. Not merely is he eating far too much and getting more portly by the week, but also he laughs uproariously at his own jokes. His last one was: 'You can always stay at the Planters' Club in Darjeeling. It's easy to get a room because all the planters are out planting.' Funny it may be, but ten minutes of laughter is a little much. And have you noticed that the only exercise he gets is when he chases flies round his tent with a fly swat?"

I called in on Drurie-Brewer. He put the tips of his fingers together. "Major," he said, "I am worried about Hargreaves. I dropped in at lunchtime the other day and there was no table in his tent; what is worse, he was eating curry with his bare hand. We oldtimers know that the East gets some people, and I fear that Hargreaves is going native."

About this time Major Thomson, known as Sparrowfart as his instructions on convoy often included the phrase "we'll start at Sparrowfart", came up to have lunch with me and to see the Track which was of great interest to everybody further back. He was horrified to find that I had parcelled all my lorries out to engineering units up and down the road. This brought them much nearer the site of their work and they all dealt direct with the Engineers who received their orders from Pat Tidy. Thomson had served in the First War and spoke of it with nostalgia — most unusual. He wore riding boots and breeches and was regarded as a bit of an ass.

"My dear Atkins," he said, "keep your company together and make a show; unless you do, you will never get the respect of your senior officers, force them to come to you for help."

"But it is far more efficient this way," I replied.

"Come, my dear fellow," he said, "what the hell are we in the Army for? Promotion, that's what matters in the long run, and you won't get promotion without making a bigger personal impact. Take my advice, put yourself first. Look at me, everyone knows me and I hear," he winked, "I'm on the list for early promotion." He was wrong. A few weeks later he was out on his ear and down to Captain, so perhaps the Army did know what it was doing.

Officers continued to be showered on me and two more now turned up: Gordon Rolfe, energetic and amusing, and a slim fair boy called James Hamilton, intelligent, well educated and well dressed, he was the only officer who had passed his Urdu exam. He had one fault: he had been so easily successful all his life that he was thoroughly spoilt and paid not the slightest attention to orders if he did not wish to obey them. His speciality with me was dumb insolence. What he needed was six months in an infantry battalion with a tough British adjutant chasing him. My officers usually ate and lived by themselves and if they had any oddity, that oddity tended to become more pronounced.

Talking of oddities, one of the problems of our unit was a boy called Poliah. He was far more girl than man and our efforts to get him to behave like a soldier were clearly doomed to failure. On Gordon Rolfe's arrival I gave instructions that Poliah was to act as his orderly. He had found his niche and took Gordon under his wing. No officer was better turned out; Rolfe's clothes were immaculately laundered and starched with rice water and his tent was always clean and decorated with flowers. Poliah stood no nonsense from anyone. If I walked in with dirty boots he would show his disapproval.

Poliah kept his *affaires* away from our unit. Once meeting him outside camp he was mincing along holding hands with a bearded Sikh. On seeing me he dodged behind the other man and kept him as a shield between us as he went past.

Later, during the surge of intense discipline that hit us I had to insist that all cooks and orderlies would wear boots, and this really upset Poliah. This was a problem for Gordon whose life was made miserable by his tearful orderly. He came up with the idea that we should open our own sick bay with Poliah in charge. We were having a lot of dysentry and Poliah was a first class nurse and really loved looking after the sick. Among them he tiptoed about in soft shoes, so that solved the boot problem.

Tim Eaton's oddity, apart from his pleasure in prophecies of disaster, was his romance with drink. Now I was in for another bout of doom.

"You remember those three Military Police at Kangpokpi, all of whom died within one week of each other of cerebral malaria." I remembered it only too well. "I have just heard that this area has got the same type of mosquito. Three days and you're dead."

"Tim," I replied, "at the first rains we will all be pulled back to Imphal where there's no malaria and anyhow, Tiddim is too high for mosquitoes."

"Ah," he replied triumphantly, "I hear on the grapevine that the stocks at Milestone 109 are far lower than planned. 17 Division will run out of food. When that happens, we will be asked to get it up to them and we will have our lorries stuck, strung out along a hundred miles of muddy road. All the men will catch malaria and we'll have the hell of a job getting them out. It will be as big a mess as last November." (That was when we were down to six fit men.)

He finished his drink and went back up the road, no doubt to sleep well, having transferred his load to me.

Chapter 2

THE TIDDIM TRACK

Colonel Towers was a man who led from the front. When he had arrived on the Tiddim Track in September 1942, it had been shingled for only seventeen miles out of Imphal and then there was a cart track up to Milestone 33; the rest was a footpath. Towers' orders were to make the road up to Tiddim by May 1st 1943. That meant another 130 miles of mountains to traverse. We had joined him in the middle of November 1942 and by this time the road was uncoiling across the hills at a speed of up to a mile a day. There were normally three bulldozers working; two would be about seven miles in front of the end of the road, one working back to us, and the other forwards. The third bulldozer was working forward at the point the road had reached. The progress Towers wanted was not less than 400 yards per bulldozer per day.

The route had to be planned and a footpath (trace) cut. The officer cutting the trace was Max Gray. He was operating with an interpreter and bags of coins with which to pay locals. There was nothing between him and the Japanese. Max was ordered by Towers to steepen his trace to a maximum rise of 1:5, as this made a shorter and quicker road. No wonder we found it difficult to get our lorries up it; 1:12 is considered steep in England but then Towers was a Cornishman and they are used to fishing villages built on cliff sides.

Shortly after we arrived, on 13th December an English Sapper named Speakman lost control of one of the bulldozers. The tracks failed to grip as he reversed and the bulldozer ran down out of control 150 feet and then went over a 20-foot cliff. As the machine fell Speakman was thrown almost clear, but his arm was caught and had to be amputated.

On 10th December Towers asked us to move his Headquarters and all his staff forward to Milestone 56. This involved lifting about two thousand men. When we started at 6.30 in the morning with every lorry we could get on the road, the track itself was a mile short of Milestone 56, but Towers decided not to change his plans. We waited with fully loaded lorries until the last cut was made through to a beautiful glade which he had chosen and which Tidy named Richmond Park. We got there and unloaded but then had the tremendous problem of getting back; we had over 100 lorries nose to tail with nowhere to turn and no passing point. I explained the problem to Towers and he asked two bulldozer drivers to go on all night. They were already extremely tired, but they cut us a big circuit on the hill and by midnight we were able to get the last lorry forward enough to let the first lorry go back down the road.

While he was with us we had few days off work. One was Christmas Day 1942 when he and Tidy arrived, both fairly drunk as this was their tenth stop, to pay us a courtesy call. He could not have come at a worse time as we were cremating one of our best VCOs. We had had a tragedy the previous day. This cremation was the only time I saw Towers off balance. After the ceremony he walked carefully to his jeep but he and Tidy had already had too many Christmas drinks and they looked pretty silly as they tried to switch their Christmas mood to suit the funeral. The episode helped me as after that I was not nervous of him and could call him Ted. Later, in 1943, Col. Towers walked through the Japanese lines into Burma accompanied only by his servant. He planned the sites of White City and Broadway for the air landings by the Chindits and then, although wounded, walked out again. He got a well-deserved DSO.

The Christmas Eve disaster had spoilt the men's holiday so we arranged for a troop of dancing girls from Imphal to come up to give a show and, in addition to our men, asked all the Indian and British officers of nearby units. This included Major Smithfield, the Engineer who was in charge of this stretch of road. To my surprise he got very drunk and later that night molested Bimola, the pretty little star of the show. I was sent for and had Smithfield, who was senior to me, forcibly carried to his tent and put under guard. After that Bimola and her mother regarded me as their trusted friend.

This problem of lack of girls was very serious but Smithfield later solved his by bringing up a nice litte Manipuri girl to live with him. She was very faithful and resisted all passes by other officers. She had nothing in common with the locals as they were not Hindus, but were Pantheists and worshipped trees, rocks and rivers. The Manipuri girls all had a good dress sense while the Kukis were the worst dressed tribe in the mountains and, unlike the Nagas, wore very drab colours.

Later, possibly in remorse for his behaviour, Smithfield asked us to arrange for another party for which he would pay and supply the drink. I duly got Bimola and her troupe up for a nautch. Her mother made one condition: Bimola, who was fourteen, was to stay in my camp not Smithfield's.

The evening came, each unit garlanded its officers sometimes with two or three ropes of flowers, and then as soon as Bimola entered, to the delight of my men, she came straight up and sang to me personally:

> 'Yours to the end of life's story,
> Yours to the far distant shore.
> How could I love anybody else,
> When I was meant to be just yours.'

My head was covered with rupee notes as the men encouraged her to bless me again and again. Another of her songs was 'The flowers of the forest are all weed awa'. In her small high voice it was quite heart-breaking. She was the most popular dancer in the area and her mother must have made a fortune. She kept her daughter absolutely chaste but at every party Bimola, to my great pleasure, came to my knee first.

At these parties the drinking was heavy among some officers. Tim tended to get aggressive when drunk and on one occasion it looked as though he was going to hit me in front of some sepoys. Gordon saw what was happening and frog-marched Tim outside where he had to sit on him to quieten him. Next morning a very penitent Tim called to apologise; he had a bad hangover and also had lost his identity card and all his money.

On 9th February we again moved the same Headquarters forward, this time to Milstone 83, where Tidy later arranged an excellent running water supply through hollow bamboos from a clear mountain spring, a spring which was the home of monster leeches, larger than any others I had seen.

The cutting of the track must be one of the engineering marvels of the century. It went so fast that our chief job was moving up towards the working face. Here we constantly met the problem of turning the vehicles. British Engineer sergeants having cut the road would, if we had no officer there at the time, order my lorries forward but never seemed to think of how we were going to get them back. To reverse twenty or thirty lorries along a recently cut mud road 12 feet wide with a fall of one hundred feet to one side was too difficult for some of the sepoys and our officers and NCOs had to do much of this reversing. By this time, however, our men had seen so many lorries fall down the khud and the driver come out unhurt that some were prepared to take the risk. It was quite extraordinary how, when the lorries rolled over and over a hundred feet or more, the steering wheel never broke loose and, as the driver instinctively hung on to it he, but not his passenger, emerged unhurt even though the cab might have been bashed in to within inches of his head. We could always pull the lorries up with the Trewhella winch. I did a bit of this myself and although with the long lever it only brought the lorries up an inch or so at a time, once they were on their wheels, which was easier to manage than one expected, they came up like lambs, or rather like gentle elephants. Unlike television, none of my lorries ever caught fire in a fall.

The Jeep Company took over where we left off and as the road lengthened all of us were kept busy servicing not only the bulldozers and the labourers (pioneer companies), but the tree clearance parties and those men engaged in bridging and blasting. Towers' theory was that everybody skilled should actually work on the road and be looked after by others. For these key workers, therefore, food and stores were run up on demand and advance camps were built for them.

Towers was now forward arranging for the cutting of the road up to the Manipur River and then right on up to Tiddim. This area came under Poom Zaman, head of the Kham How Chins. Towers persuaded him to leave the year's agricultural work undone and to put everybody, for pay of course, on the road. The Chins were promised sufficient food to take the place of the harvest. I am glad to say we just managed to fulfil this promise, but it was a close thing.

Poom fancied himself as an engineer as he and his father had built many suspension bridges across the streams in the Chin hills. The longest of these was over the Manipur River and was 300 feet long. Towers told me that he was horrified to see that while one main rope was 2 inches in diameter the other main one was only 1½ inches.

"Tell me, Chief," he asked, "why are these ropes different sizes?"

"I think they should both be the larger size," said Poom, through an interpreter, "but I had run out of money when I bought the second rope and you get lots more rope for fewer rupees if it's thinner. I do not think it's very safe."

"How did you know it was all right when you had built it?" asked Towers.

"I sent one mule across and watched, then two mules across, then three mules, and when four mules were on the bridge together, the right-hand rope started to stretch, so I ordered that it be a three-mule bridge."

"If it had broken," said Towers, "wouldn't that have been very expensive for you? Mules aren't cheap."

"I would not be so silly as to send my own mules, Sahib," replied the Chief. "I borrowed them from the stables of the Deputy Commissioner at Tiddim when he was away."

By the middle of March plans had been made for re-bridging the Manipur River. Concrete was needed for the end supports. Concrete is packed in paper sacks weighing 112 lbs, and the most a mule can carry is one maund, which is 82 lbs. We brought the concrete to the road head and here the bags were split and repacked in jute sacks. The weather was dry so the column of mules started off in good fettle. On the twenty-mile journey the mules began to sweat. By the time they reached the river each mule was in a concrete waistcoat. The bags could not be unloaded and there were no other bags into which to load such concrete as was still dry. It was miserable chaos for two days with everyone made more on edge by the great unrest among the mules. These could not bray as all war mules are silenced but a mule can sulk like mad. Concrete won't wash off and you can't break it off a mule's back. In the end it took some weeks to clear as the concrete was gradually shed with the mules' hair, but we had some bald and bad tempered mules about for some time.

Meanwhile the building of the bridge went on apace and the

first jeep went across on 26th April. This bridge was 17 Division's vital link with the outside world. On their retreat in March 1944, 16,000 men, 2,500 vehicles and guns, and 3,500 animals went across it in eight days, and if the Japanese had captured and blown it Imphal might have fallen and then perhaps India.

During the building of the road my own Company camped at fourteen different sites on the Track between Milestones 17 and 83. Every one of these was a beautiful glade or shelf in the mountains. Pine trees flourished at over five thousand feet together with rhododendrons, and lower down there were oaks and almost all the European trees. The neem tree was particularly valued by our men as from it you can get twigs which, when frayed at the end, can be used as toothbrushes. Indians take great care of their teeth.

There were very few wild animals about because the tremendous activity along this thin line of road had driven them away. From the miles of jungle all around we must have been watched by tigers and deer. At night one could hear the deer barking. In these mountains the ground area was so dominated by trees that there was little grass growing and as a result there were no grazing animals. Barking deer browse on leaves, so they could flourish. When Pat Tidy was out trying to shoot deer for the mess, he came on a grass clearing in which lay a number of human skulls in a circle. The Chins would not follow him there, and neither would his men. At night, it felt as if we were in Kipling's 'oldest lands', of which he wrote:

> 'A stone's throw out on either hand,
> From the well ordered road we tread
> And all the world is wild and strange
> Ghost and Ghoul and Djinn and Sprite
> Shall bear us company tonight
> For we have reached the oldest lands
> Wherein the powers of darkness range.'

Even so, it was a happy and healthy time during the course of which we came under the command of Lt.-Col. Tarver. I was responsible to Tarver of my own Corps in the same way as a RE commanding officer would be responsible to a Lt.-Col. in his Corps, but the operational orders continued to come from Towers.

Tarver announced that he was coming to stay with me for a week. That is an awfully long time. Guests and fish go off in three days and I did not welcome the prospect of his visit. He arrived; small, energetic, clear-spoken and amusing. The first day he did not start drinking until six o'clock, but by seven o'clock had finished a bottle of rum. Next morning he surfaced at half past nine, ate a hearty breakfast, inspected one of my platoons, gave us some excellent advice and started drinking again at twelve. At four o'clock he surfaced again, inspected my workshop platoon and started drinking at half past five. Christie, his staff captain had, I later learned, been given instructions from above to stop his colonel drinking. I now began to see why Tarver had decided to stay with me for seven days. With the cunning of the alcoholic he had left his staff captain a great deal of work to do at Palel and scarpered across to drink with us.

After the second day of the visit I wondered how I would get through the week. I could drink no more. I then had the brilliant, but possibly unkind idea of sending him up to stay with Tim where they could both mess with Col. Towers. This worked well, except that Tim and Col. Tarver rarely got to the mess in the evening. Instead they had a special curry and some bottles of rum. They missed something by not going to Towers' mess as Tidy had arranged for fresh fish to be killed in the Manipur River. He used a safety fuse, detonator and gun cotton, which was safer than a grenade. Towers was very food conscious and had Tidy write bitter letters to Corps HQ about the lack of vegetables. HQ sent him up from Imphal packets of onion, pea and radish seeds and told him to grow his own. Tidy planted but never harvested them. Perhaps parts of the mountains are now overrun with onions and peas gone rampant.

Tidy also went back and got some rather thin live ducks from the Imphal depot. He arrived with them in triumph and decided to fatten them up on our hard biscuits. There was a flooded slit trench nearby so he had the ducks tied by the leg, fed them and launched them into the trench. They quacked madly and sank. He pulled them up by the strings before they drowned. While they fattened on dry land he puzzled over their lack of buoyancy. The solution he uncovered was that they had travelled up from Dimapur to Imphal in a lorry half full of cans of petrol which had leaked. The ducks had become degreased.

Tidy was detailed off by Towers to do the social drinking with Poom. Poom's tipple was fermented millet known as zou. This was drunk in a group out of a gourd using only one straw. Poom's elderly mother with toothless gums shared the straw with Tidy and the others; he did not enjoy these parties.

Returning to Tarver, I thought he had been instructed to send in a confidential report on my company and I was torn between the duty to stop him drinking and the feeling that he would write a more amiable report if he was allowed to continue. For the last two days he came down and stayed with me and took the chance to go through my officer position. I was astonished to find out how much he knew, and for the first time I realised what a bad reputation my platoon in Palel had acquired. Before Tarver had come out to us he had investigated some fierce complaints about its work and he had discussed Johnson with the local Engineers. He had now made up his mind to move him out as a subaltern to another company. He had come up with the view that both Johnson and I would have to go but he had found that our company on the Track had a first class reputation and he had now made his decision. When he got back to Palel he acted on it at once and the terrible weight of having a second-in-command whom I distrusted was suddenly and unexpectedly taken off my back.

The last night Tarver and I were asked out to an Engineer's party. It was a good evening and his driver brought us back in the staff car. To reach our Headquarters guardroom we had to walk forty or fifty yards along a path and across a small stream. Flashing my torch on all the obstructions and talking as I went, I escorted Tarver with the exaggerated care of the partly drunk. We reached the guardroom and the standard routine began:

"Turn out the guard," shouted the Malayali sepoy in the English that was used in the Indian Army for this purpose only.

"Guard turn out," shouted the guard commander in reply and all the sepoys bundled out of the guard tent and lined up. The Subahdar had seen they were especially immaculate because he was expecting the Colonel's inspection. I stood to attention and waited for Colonel Tarver to inspect the guard. Nothing happened. I turned around; the Colonel was not there. I looked all around, it was like magic, he had vanished into thin air. I took the guard commander, Naik Daya Ram, with me and we found Tarver some twenty yards back, sitting happily in the stream with his legs in the air. He had fallen off the footbridge. Daya Ram on my instructions picked him up in his strong arms and we returned together to the guard which I inspected myself and dismissed. Daya Ram then carried the Colonel to his tent where his own orderly took over. This episode was not mentioned between us again.

The last thing the Colonel did before he left us was to ask for a pair of sepoy's boots. We all wore them and the Quartermaster quickly fitted him up. He was due to be charged personally for this and the paperwork went through. Shortly afterwards, however, Tarver died suddenly in his sleep and I cancelled the charge. This was to be brought up again two years later when I was up before a Court of Enquiry (a preliminary to a possible Court Martial) for misuse of Government property.

Tarver was the last of the odd colonels we were to have. The next few months were to see crowns and stars falling like autumn leaves, as discipline tightened fiercely and all weak links were eliminated. But I liked Tarver, he had once been a good officer and he was helpful to me. If his family should read this book I would be sorry if it upsets them but I have not changed his name, as I have changed some others.

After Tarver left we were told we could have two days off at Easter and informed that on the Saturday there was going to be a special treat. A film unit had come up from Calcutta and was giving shows all along the Burma front. Any break in the monotony was welcome and with great enthusiasm we arranged to take all the men who could be spared; there was going to be enough room in the clearing for over a thousand soldiers. Colonel Towers had arranged a drink for everyone so he must have been illegally storing up our rations of rum for some time, but then he never took any notice of army orders.

A big white screen was erected on the side of the clearing and we all sat down, the Indians on the ground, and behind them the officers in the folding camp chairs we had all brought with us. There was a great air of festivity. Then the film started. It was about a yellow fever epidemic in the jungle. In front of us appeared on the screen numbers of sick and dying men, a condition with which we were only too familiar. In the midst of this chaos an American doctor and a pretty girl fought desperately to keep everybody alive. It was terribly depressing and could not have been a more unsuitable film. Next day the officers were besieged with questions from the men as to whether or not it was true that yellow fever was coming here. After all we had malaria, typhus and cholera already, and perhaps last night's film was just a warning of what was coming.

Recently I was telling a friend about this and he capped the story. In 1944, when he was in charge of reinforcements due to be flown into Burma, they had a special treat on their last evening — a film show. It was a story of an air crash in the mountains. In eight hours time they would be flying across some of the wildest mountains in the world. Who was responsible for choosing these extraordinarily inappropriate films we never heard.

On Easter Sunday I knew that all my lorries were off the Track and also that there were no other vehicles working. The mud road had been recently scraped flat and was like good tarmac to drive on. I went down in my 15-cwt long-nosed Chevrolet to see Hargreaves and was going flat out, enjoying the unusual surface and the empty road, when round a corner I met Paddy going flat out and coming up to see me. We both swerved to the left, but our offside mudguards were badly bashed. We limped back with the two 15-cwt trucks to Headquarters where Sub-Conductor Snowden, whose workshop was already full with other repairs, clearly thought that we had both been pretty bloody silly. He made sure that neither 15-cwt was repaired for over two weeks. I took my lesson without pushing him. Meanwhile I had to use my station wagon, which had just arrived and which I did not like, and poor Paddy had to use a 3-ton lorry. I think Snowden, who would never commit himself, enjoyed the situation.

"Tell me, Sub-Conductor, when can I have my 15-cwt back?"

"It's very tricky, it all depends on spare parts, spare parts for 15-cwts are very tricky, but you will have it as soon as it's ready sir."

"By the way Conductor, while you are here, we now have 40 lorries off the road. How many of them can you repair in the next two weeks?"

"Well, sir, that really is a tricky question, very tricky indeed. It all depends."

"Depends on what, Conductor?"

"Depends on when we get them repaired sir. You will understand it's all very tricky."

Later in the day I asked Sergeant Goodbury the same question about my 15-cwt. He scratched his head.

"I don't rightly know, sir, I've put a real good nigger onto it."

"Don't call them niggers, Sergeant, they are Indians not niggers."

The two of them would never give an estimate of time.

One of the reasons the long-nosed Chevrolet was so much more popular than the Ford was that it was light on steering and its petrol pump, which pushed petrol upwards, had a glass bowl in which one could easily see any water or dirt. It was therefore very easy to clear any petrol blockage.

Chapter 3

THE VEGETABLE FRAUD

With the improved health of everyone up the Tiddim Track there came additional energy which showed itself in some strange ways. One of these was the vegetable fraud.

Jemadar Rudolf, a missionary educated Punjabi, had, despite serious fever, kept going energetically throughout the crisis months of 1942. He was now fully recovered. I had a suspicion that he was selling blankets and trousers to the hill tribes, which in this area were Kukis, but as he was a Viceroy Commissioned Officer (VCO) he had many rights, even more than a KCO and I could not act without a clear case. Rudolf was not only physically powerful, he was also intelligent, well-mannered and ruthless. There was little chance of getting any evidence against him. In India rumours fly fast — try and pin down some fact for court martial or a legal case and there is nothing to be found when one needs it, particularly against a man like Rudolf.

My suspicions were confirmed when, for the cold weather, we all got excellent new chain-knit jerseys. I was astonished to see them within a few days being worn in the Kuki village. A check on the company stores and records showed that no jerseys were missing but in the meantime some forty men had gone on leave. When they returned without jerseys I interviewed them all one by one in the orderly room tent and gradually it emerged that some of them had sold their jerseys to Jemadar Rudolf for ten rupees each. When pressed there was no firm evidence as they all then said that perhaps they had misunderstood the question and in fact they now remembered that the jerseys had been stolen while they were on leave.

I decided, rather naively perhaps, to give Jemadar Rudolf a new job, one which would keep him apart from the men. I therefore put him on the 'vegetable run' which Towers had arranged. He was required to drive back each morning to Imphal, load his lorry with the vegetables which the local purchasing officer was buying in quantity from the market there, then, with his truck full of cabbages, cauliflowers, ladies' fingers, corn-on-the-cob and potatoes, drive seventy miles back up the road, making many deliveries en route. He had a list of the quantity of vegetables he was to deliver to each unit and these orders he meticulously fulfilled. There were, however, good cabbages and bad ones, worm-eaten cauliflowers and firm ones, and I learned later that he pulled off the road at Bishenpur and re-sorted his load. Gordon Rolfe who was most amused by the whole episode found out how Rudolf made his killing. Leaving a pile of excellent vegetables well in sight, he would start handing over a pile of miserable vegetables to the Quartermaster of some unit. The conversation might go like this:

"Could we not have some of those good cabbages, Jemadar Sahib?"

"I would like to let you have them, Quartermaster Sahib, but they are for my good friends in other companies to whom I owe duty."

After two or three days of this the Quartermaster might say, "Tell me, Jemadar Sahib, how is it that so many other companies are your good friends?"

"I cannot think why," replied Jemadar Rudolf, "but they much like me and often for my good work they give presents — perhaps bottle of gin or whisky or maybe good torch. They tell me they look on me as good friend. Cigarettes also are welcome presents at all times."

By this means Jemadar Rudolf amassed a supply of highly barterable and saleable articles without selling a single vegetable. I knew nothing of this at the time and anyhow no one else in the company would have had the energy to make this long run of over a hundred miles a day and also ensure that his lorry was always in good order.

Meanwhile Colonel Towers was still driving our extraordinary road forward at the rate of one mile per day and to do so all the best machinery was needed right up in the front. Further back Major Smithfield was responsible to Towers for the first fifty miles near Imphal. He was engaged in ironing out the corners and in strengthening the road surface. When one of Colonel Towers' bulldozers broke down he ordered Smithfield to send him up the only one he had for his own use. Smithfield sent it up with a bitter note: 'All I now have left with which to maintain a fifty-mile stretch of road is twenty-four wheelbarrows.' Towers at once sent down one of my lorries with the reply: 'I had no idea you had so many wheelbarrows. Please hand over to the bearer of this note sixteen of them. Your pioneers can use wicker baskets.'

Towers had some justification because when making a mountain road, it is the foremost point which is the most difficult to service and drive forward.

On issue all our lorries had been equipped with excellent petrol strainers but, during the days of chaos in 1942, most of these had been deliberately punctured by the drivers in order to get the petrol through more quickly. Nearly all the petrol cans in the dumps leaked so whenever it rained water got into the cans and from there into our tanks. We now treasured the few petrol strainers which were still in good condition. It made filling up difficult as they had to be shared around.

We were also short of petrol pump washers. The Chevrolet washer was no use to us and there were no Ford washers anywhere. In order to keep the air out we used to make balls of dough with atta and water, and plaster these all over the pump. Cakes of soap would do the same job. I tried all sorts of ways to get cork washers for the lorries. In the end I wired 4-Corps HQ to ask them to air-lift 400 cork washers from Canada where the lorries had been made. Nothing ever arrived so the order must have got tangled up in various bureaucratic offices. In the end I had some soft leather jerkins cut up to take their place. This was of course against the regulations but they were a bit better than the cigarette packets which up till then we had used for the same purpose.

The only big lorries on the Tiddim Track were mine and now that they had done over 3,000 miles the metal in their pistons, which I am sure was made of the wrong grade of steel, was wearing out. One could stand on the high mountain passes with the Tiddim Track curling and dipping in both directions across the hills and down into the jungle and, wherever a lorry was working, a thin column of blue smoke moved above it pinpointing its position — there would on a clear day be fifty or sixty moving pillars of smoke. The engines in these lorries were the ordinary

Ford V8 as used in cars and 15-cwts. In addition to being badly made they had no extra power with which to cope with our 3-ton steel-bodied lorries, let alone with the load.

In the workshops we were getting on top of many of the minor troubles, but the engines defeated us. We needed new ones and that year we were never to get more than a dozen. Then there were the batteries. To every twenty lorries we only had one battery capable of starting an engine so every morning we had heartbreaking starts with the one lorry with a good battery towing the others. An inexpert driver, when his lorry started, would often run into the back of the towing lorry, so many radiators were damaged. Snowden would cut out portions of the damaged radiators and the bad cells of the faulty batteries and by this means we kept them going. Once started the engine could not be turned off all day unless the lorry stopped on a slope.

On these hills we used all eight gears constantly and many of our inexperienced drivers slipped their clutches far more than was necessary and now the clutches began to wear out. At Snowden's request I spent a great deal of time visiting other workshops as far away as Dimapur and I had soon cleared the whole area out of all their stocks of Ford clutch plates.

The footbrakes were now not too bad but we had not got round to adjusting the handbrakes. On one occasion I came round a bend to find a lorry on a steep hill blocking the road. The driver was sitting motionless in the cab.

"What is trouble? Why does your lorry sit here making trouble for the road?"

"Engine is bad, sahib, and has died."

"Get down and I will try," I said.

"It is not possible for me to get down, sahib. The handbrake is bad. It has been dead many days. Much trouble for me but Havildar Sahib does not listen. It is always an order, 'go out quickly — go out, go out.'"

I blocked the lorry's four wheels with rocks, got it started and gave him a note back to Tim Eaton.

"Slowly, slowly, go back home," I told the driver. "My chitty tells Eaton sahib that the lorry is bad."

Communication continued to be a tremendous problem. This sepoy and I were both talking Urdu, a language foreign to us both, so the opportunities for misunderstandings were frequent. One of the stories on the Track — I never knew whether or not it was true — showed this. A duty Havildar reported to his Captain:

"Sahib, the guard commander holds in his tent a hillman caught stealing a blanket. Wouldst thou see him now?"

"Not now," replied the Captain. "Take the blanket from him so that he will lie cold (tanda) in the night. I will see him when he is stiff with cold in the morning."

In the morning the Captain asked for the hillman to be brought before him.

"Bad news, sahib," replied the Indian adjutant. "Guard commander shot him last night. He says he did this on your orders."

'Tanda', translated from colloquial Urdu to Pushtu and then on into one of the dialects, had come out 'cold and dead' instead of 'stiff with cold'.

The monsoon was approaching and before we moved back to Imphal I considered the problem of VD, of which we had had so much in India. We'd now mastered the technique of explaining to the men the purpose of and how to put on french letters (one demonstrated with a stick), but now the safer Early Treatment packets were issued to all units. These were a little more complicated as they involved the use of a protective ointment as well as the condom. As the VCOs were too embarrassed to explain it to the men, it fell again to the KCOs to carry out this task, which they duly did.

I went down to see the Area Commander to get my new orders. He gave me a pleasant welcome and lunch. I asked him if we could set up an approved brothel, medically inspected. The men had hardly seen a girl for four months and the Manipuri girls were pretty and had roving eyes, but VD was rife. In the past, approved brothels had been a regular feature of the Army in India, but this had been stopped by one of the Viceroy's wives — I think Lady Willingdon. My request caused some amusement.

When we did get back to Imphal our training had evidently been successful and we had hardly any more cases. It is a chargeable offence to catch VD in the Army, and it goes down in a man's record. In India it was a very serious cause of casualties, and I see that in 1945 British troops had a rate of 7.2%, while Indians only had 4.6%. The Japanese dealt with the problem differently. They shipped in 'comfort' girls who were bought in mainly from Korea for the sum of 1000 yen each. A girl was credited with 2 yen for half an hour with a soldier, and was free to leave after 500 men, by which time she had earned her purchase money. Many seemed to have enjoyed their lives and stayed on and were well looked after. There was a ration scale of one girl per 40 men. In defeat, some of the girls committed suicide beside the Japanese troops. The system worked well and as condoms had to be worn, VD in the Japanese army was almost eradicated.

It took two of our officers and also Sub-Conductor Snowden and Sergeant Goodbury to bring back to Imphal all the weak compression lorries which were stuck strung out along seventy miles of road. They had to be got in before the monsoon but they were only able to average fifteen miles a day in a twelve-hour stint. Up the steep hills every poor lorry had to be helped by a good one. Going as fast as they could on the flat, the convoy could sometimes reach five miles an hour. After the first day of the move I was asked by Corps how long we would be on the job, as our convoys were slowing down the flow of traffic up to Tiddim.

I drove up that evening and found the first group camped with Snowden and Sergeant Minnit. They looked very cosy sitting beside the fire with the drivers gathered around and the firelight flickering on the foliage of the trees above them. Sergeant Minnit, by the light of a hurricane lamp, was writing a letter home. I sat down, was brought a mug of scalding sweet tea and chatted for a bit.

"When do you think you'll get these lorries into Imphal, Conductor?"

"Well, sir, that all depends, a tricky question that is."

"Depends on what?"

"Depends on how fast we go," replied Conductor Snowden. I think he thought that a reasonable reply and perhaps it was with such a batch of old crocks.

After I finished the tea I drove back up the road to where Paddy Hargreaves and Sergeant Goodbury were encamped. Another cosy site, another flickering fire, another scalding cup of sweet tea. I interrupted Sergeant Goodbury putting rancid coconut oil on his bald spot. He was a great believer in the efficacy of this but could rarely use it because of the smell.

"Tell me, Sergeant, when do you think you will get this lot into Imphal?"

"I can't rightly say, sir," replied the Sergeant. "Some of these lorries are right buggers, so I can't rightly say, sir, but we've got some good niggers on the job. Still, I can't rightly say sir."

Paddy Hargreaves came out of his tent and offered me a weak pink gin which I refused. I asked him the same question.

"Well, Major," he drawled in the western style he affected, "the redskins are restless tonight, but you can rely on us to get through — yes Sir, we'll get through."

Hargreaves was posted away shortly afterwards and we all missed him.

Further back still, Gordon Rolfe and Tim Eaton were camped together. In front of their fire their orderlies had put out camp chairs and a table. Nearby a tent had been erected. On the camp beds the sheets had already been turned down by Poliah, and the mosquito nets were up. They had both bathed and had finished dinner. Tim's orderly now brought me hot water in a basin and a towel. I washed, sat down, and Tim poured me a strong rum and orange. There was almost a full moon and the insect bats were out flitting between the trees while the large fruit bats were feeding in a Karnikar tree. This tree grows up to the 4,000-feet level. I wondered what the bats found to eat there as it was too early in May for fruit, but evidently they like nectar. The high-pitched hum of a mosquito sounded danger in my ears and I re-applied mosquito cream on my wrists, forehead, ears and the back of the neck.

There was a companionable silence as we listened to the noises of the jungle. From the distance a deer barked and was answered. I stirred myself.

"Corps want to know when we'll get our lorries in. When do you think, Tim?"

Tim, who had no opinion of the staff, replied, "When we bloody get there."

"Well, I'll say tomorrow then." I pitched it short enough to stir Tim to a reply.

"We'll be lucky if we're back in two days and it might be three," said Tim, and Gordon nodded. I signalled Corps next morning and told them three days but in fact we were back in two.

When I got to Imphal, Drurie had finished allocating each platoon's quarters. This was far more complicated in Imphal than elsewhere as the huts and clearings had each to be requisitioned and paid for by the Army.

Workshops were to be stationed up the road past Headquarters. All the platoons had moved in and the next day Sergeant Goodbury who was the first to arrive with part of the workshop staff, reported to me.

"Where do we go sir?" he asked.

"I don't rightly know, Sergeant. Mr Drurie-Brewer has the details."

"Where will I find him, sir?"

"I can't rightly say, Sergeant. Have a cup of char while you're waiting."

After a few minutes Conductor Snowden came in.

"We made better time than we expected sir. Where do we go?"

"It all depends Conductor. It is all rather tricky, so it all depends."

"Depends on what, sir?"

"Depends on where you have been placed by Mr Drurie-Brewer."

Snowden suddenly got the point, and grinned.

"I'm sorry, sir, we did rather play you up about the convoy. It won't happen again."

The last thirty miles into Imphal was on a raised road between rice fields and on that the lorries made good progress. They were now coming in fast and the very last four lorries were brought in by Gordon Rolfe. He arrived in at 7 o'clock in the evening, very tired but pleased with himself. He was wearing our regular daytime uniform of shorts and shirt with short sleeves. He reminded me recently that the conversation went like this:

"That's the lot of them, sir. They are all in."

"Why, Rolfe, are you wearing shorts after 6 o'clock in the evening?"

"Well, we've had a very hard day, sir."

"You had all your kit with you, so did your men. Why did you not stop and change?"

"We were trying to get in before nightfall. Our lights are very poor."

"Do you realise, Rolfe, that it is a very serious offence for an officer to be in shorts after 6 o'clock. You have put the health of yourself and your men at risk."

Forty years later that conversation still rankles with Gordon, but of course for me the debacle of 1942, when I lost 99.75% of my men sick in twelve weeks, was dominant in my mind. In Rolfe's mind, malaria did not have the same impact. Incidentally, he had driven through Bishenpur, fifteen miles from Imphal, where malaria-carrying anopheles mosquitoes were rampant as the road lay under the hills. The local type of anopheles could only breed in streams running down from the mountains.

Chapter 4

THE MONSOON

Three platoons and Headquarters were now back in Imphal for the rainy season. The monsoon when it came was solid and unrelenting. It would rain sometimes for a week on end at five inches a day; everything was damp and mould grew on one's boots and on one's hairbrush.

I was slow in withdrawing the fourth platoon as the Engineers asked me to leave it up there. With the rain came malaria and three weeks later there were only ten fit men and ninety were ill. It was a bitter reminder of malaria's power. When they came back, once again the rank smell of fever clung to them all and many had to be carried out of their lorries.

I now came under the command of Lt.-Col. (Biscuit) Singh. I forget his full name, but he was a tall, good-looking Sikh, well educated and with a regular commission. At Sandhurst, probably to avoid offending his own conscience, he had, instead of using the normal swear words, gradually adapted the use of the then current expressions of 'It takes the biscuit' and 'hard cheese' into 'Oh, my cheese and biscuits!' This earned him the affectionate nickname of 'Biscuit Singh', which still clung to him. He did not seem to have any religious restrictions and was a pleasant guest and a firm commander. When he went back to India I never heard of him again, but he should have risen high when independence came. He was the second Indian I had served under.

We were not to be left in peace for long. As Tim had forecast, the fighting units right at the head of the road ran out of food. We were ordered to load up with supplies and send men up as far as they could get. Each man was given a week's rations and they drove until they bogged down in the mud. 17 Division sent down some winch lorries to get them past the worst points. A few of the lorries got as far as 90 miles up the mud track before they finally came to a halt. They were stuck there for up to two weeks before a break in the wet weather enabled us to recover them. Every man in that convoy got malaria and three of them died. All our officers were involved in the recovery of the vehicles and the drivers when reached were wrapped in extra blankets. They were a very ill group when we had them carried to their tents on their return. Unlike November 1942, when the medical services had completely collapsed and it was a death sentence to send a man to hospital, now we had good medical support close by in Imphal.

The extraordinary thing about the Imphal plain was that although full of mosquitoes, none were anopheles except within half a mile of the mountains. As a result the town itself was malaria-free and so were the Manipuri villages which were all located at least half a mile from the foot of the hills.

The company had been given good quarters in bashas among the criss-cross of ditches and small paddocks which, with their big bamboo hedges, made up the town of Imphal. Over half a million people lived in this flat plain with the water table during the monsoon only eighteen inches below the surface. The population used shallow trench latrines in which flies bred like mad. The only drainage of the sewage was into the sluggish river. The place was unbelievably fertile and to catch fish one merely had to put two dams across a ditch and bail out the water. One of the fish on sale in the market was the ugly black catfish with big whiskers. It could lie dormant in mud in the dry season.

We were pleased with the site, but no sooner had we arrived than cholera struck. There was only enough serum for the Army and none to spare for the local population, which started dying all around us. At any one time two or three cremation fires might be burning within two hundred yards of my Headquarters. All of us were inoculated and were told it was effective for three months, but we were doubtful if we were safe. Now we added fear of flies to our fear of mosquitoes and of the long grass which so often carried scrub typhus mites.

To reduce the risk of infection we brought in strict eating disciplines. After cooking, all food was immediately put under mosquito nets. The men lined up close by the nets to fetch their food which was served directly from under the net onto their mess tins. If one saw a fly land for a moment on a grain of rice one knew that that grain probably carried cholera. This I can assure you takes away from the pleasure of eating. I was particularly aware of the danger as my grandmother Elizabeth had died of cholera in Calcutta. My grandparents had dined with friends and although slightly flushed Elizabeth was all right at dinner. She died in the night. Before breakfast the next morning my grandfather called round to his friends, distraught. It was one of the saddest family stories of my youth and was made particularly poignant as my grandmother was due to sail next day for England where my mother and my uncle, both in their early teens, were longing to see her. My grandmother's grave is in the same cemetery as that of Rose Aylmer, who died so young, and of whom the poet Landor wrote:

> 'Ah, what avails the sceptred race!
> Ah, what the form divine!
> When every virtue, every grace!
> Rose Aylmer, all were thine.'

In the middle of the cholera epidemic we had a rabies scare. A dog in a nearby compound got rabies, ran amok and was shot near the officers' mess. Just before this I had adopted a stray dog, Rags, an appealing black and grey mongrel. A RAMC Major arrived to check the area and finding I had a dog told me I must shoot it. This was only one of the precautions we had to take. All the mess staff and all the officers had to be injected. The full course at that time was twenty-four large injections in the skin of the stomach. All of us were thin and this daily injection of fluid into skin which had no fat around it was most painful; our stomachs became yellow and black with bruising. Our mess cook, after his first injection, refused to go for the second one. I put him under close arrest for twenty-four days and each day he was carried forcibly to the doctor to receive his injection. The episode amused the rest of the company.

I was very upset about Rags but knew it was necessary to carry out the instructions to kill him. I took him off to the foothills with my pistol and I am sure he sensed what I intended to do. I am now convinced that dogs can read one's mind. On an occasion recently when we had to put down one of our family dogs, we made the mistake of talking about it in front of him. He sat there shivering; he knew. Rags also knew, and he struggled so fiercely to escape that he disturbed my aim and I had to shoot him three times before he was dead. I was most upset that I had given him so much pain. On the way back my driver, who regarded himself as privileged, remarked:

"Very strange people, sahibs. That dog not ill, he quite well. Why feed dog for many weeks and like him very much and then bang, bang, shoot him when he is quite well."

I was too upset to try and explain.

We had come back from our happy and wild life on the Tiddim Track where we had not been troubled either by the enemy or by generals, to find a new attitude. The Army was disciplining itself and although it made life very uncomfortable it was all too necessary. Churchill said: "On the declaration of war some strange companions take their seats at the Council Board, antiquated officers, incompetent commanders, hostile neutrals, malignant fortunes, awful miscalculations." Our army showed the effect of all of them.

One of the reasons for the failure of the Army, and it had failed, was trouble at the top. I am a great admirer of Wavell but the responsibilities which had landed on his broad shoulders had, in retrospect, been too much for him. After the first failures in Burma he had appointed his Chief of Staff Lt.-General Hutton to command the army but when Hutton failed to hold the Japanese advance, Wavell lost his cool and railed at him in public. It was most embarrassing and most unlike him. Then a few days later Wavell sacked the 17 Divisional Commander, Major-General Smythe VC, out of hand, and reduced him in rank. Cowan was appointed to the Division and he held this command for some years. Later Hutton was also sacked and replaced by Lt.-General Alexander but Hutton was required to stay on as Alexander's Chief of Staff, a very difficult task, which he carried out well.

By the only fortunate chance of the withdrawal General Slim, the Corps Commander, was from 1/6 Gurkhas and both his Divisional Commanders were from the same battalion. They were friends of twenty years standing and were able, over the open radio, to talk in their own personal code. They used a mixture of Gurkali and bits out of their shared past, which confused the Japanese. What is it about the Gurkhas that made their British officers rise to such heights of courage and tenacity? To have been a Gurkha officer is a proud boast.

In India Lt.-General Irwin was commanding the front and he thought the army in Burma had failed, which in part it had. When Lt.-General Slim handed the badly mauled troops over to him, Irwin was quite extraordinarily rude to him.

Irwin did not trust any of his Major-Generals or Brigadiers or indeed any ranks in the army. He wrote: 'It is monstrous that I have at times been forced to undertake the duties which should properly be carried out by Divisional, Brigade and even Battalion Commanders. What is worse is that the majority of Battalion Commanders have little or no confidence in their men.'

It was too true. Both British and Indian soldiers, even of some of the best regiments, had lost their morale, were terrified of the Japanese, and for a short and terrible time could not be relied upon to obey orders. However there was a change coming. With the full support of Wavell, on 13th February 1943, Wingate launched 'Longcloth', his first Chindit expedition which slipped past the Japanese and across the Chindwin. I saw them going up the Palel Road,* horses, mules, Gurkhas and a number of British soldiers from the 13th King's Battalion which had been raised in Liverpool. These English soldiers were almost as small as the Gurkhas. Wingate had given the King's Battalion very fierce field training, and in the course of it he had sacked the colonel and thrown out 250 men. He went in on foot with the remains of that battalion, the 3rd/2nd Gurkha Rifles,** and support troops. The total force of 3,000 men was divided into eight columns each commanded by a major and each having 15 horses and 100 mules. They were to have a very rough time but at least went in thoroughly well fed. An old friend of mine, Bruce Rust, was given the job of supplying their rations as they came up the road. He knew the area well as in July 1942 he had commanded 'The Impressed Transport Company' made up of civilian drivers; these had all deserted when the Japanese bombed Imphal. Now his contacts enabled him to get hold of enough ducks to give all the columns a special treat.

Before they went in, Wingate issued an extraordinary Order of the Day, extracts of which read as follows:

---

*The long journey of 180 miles on foot, by night treks, from Dimapur to Tamu, was quite unnecessary and much resented.

**Captain Henry Birtwistle, then adjutant of the 3rd/2nd, tells me that the battalion, both officers and Gurkhas, had no love for Wingate. They did not consider him a good leader.

'Today we are on the threshold of battle. Victory cannot be counted on but we shall go forward determined to do what we can for our comrades in arms and resolved to do the right. Knowing the vanity of man's effort, let us pray God may accept our services and direct our endeavours.'

I wonder what the Liverpudlians made of that, but it did put war on to a different level and a soldier needs to believe in his cause.

The Chindits were in Burma behind the Japanese for almost four months and 2,182 men, far more than expected, tottered out in June exhausted, sick and emaciated. They had not achieved much in terms of warfare, but the morale effect on the whole army was quite astonishing. Rumours about their successes went up and down the Road and grew at each telling. On the Road and in Imphal we had no girls, no papers, and few books, so we gossiped like a village. Everything of any interest was chewed over and discussed and re-discussed over the rum with which by my grandiose mistake in Delhi I had swamped the Army.

Meanwhile, under pressure from above, I was tightening discipline day by day. Havildar Clerk Kuttapan Nair asked to speak to me officially. He said that all the Havildars felt I was asking too much of them. There was no doubt that the pressure everywhere was a great trial to all of us, including our new Colonel, but the Army had nothing else to do during the monsoon rains except to get itself into proper order for the battle to come. Inspections by senior officers were all too frequent. We had all the peacetime bull but none of the peacetime amusements.

One thing was taken off my shoulders. Lt.-Col. Singh had instructions from high up to test my lorries; clearly someone did not believe my reports that they had no power. He arrived unexpectedly and had ten lorries, chosen at random, lined up. He then drove each one himself along the dead flat track outside our lines. With his foot hard down and the lorries empty, four out of the ten had a maximum speed of under 5 mph and the others did not do very much better. He was convinced and reported back that our lorries were useless without new engines. From that time forward we gradually had those ghastly steel Fords replaced but only in dribs and drabs, and then by other Fords but with wooden bodies.

Already Tim Eaton and others who had been with me during the disastrous autumn of the previous year were looking back at

1942 with nostalgia. The stories of those terrible days did not need elaboration; it was engraved deep in everyone's memory.

Now that we were fully re-established as a reliable unit I gave a formal dinner party to which all my officers and Colonel Singh came; I also invited the three British workshop NCOs. I used up all my own two months' supply of whisky, which was a much appreciated change from the rum. Our cook made an excellent fish pie from tinned salmon; this was regarded as a great treat instead of the curry and the roast goat which was our normal fare.

After this Colonel Singh used to come down quite often to play pontoon (*vingt-et-un*) with us. He was a good player and once or twice won heavily — say £50 in a night, and on these occasions he was very reluctant to take the money. I had been brought up in a hard gambling school by my two elderly great aunts in the New Forest. They always played with us children for money and expected to pay or be paid promptly: no excuses were accepted.

"However hard up you are David," Great Aunt Nelly used to say, "pay your gambling debts first, they are debts of honour: your tailor and the tradesmen can wait." Unexpected advice from two spinsters. I insisted, therefore, that Colonel Singh should take the money; if he did not do so we could not play with him again.

Early independence for India was now the accepted idea in Delhi and the Indian Army was racially conscious only in that it was constantly looking for Indian Officers to promote. The army started the war with 1,010 Indian KCOs and ended with 15,740, enough to officer the whole peacetime army. On occasions directives came out insisting that no King's Commissioned Officer should ever be referred to as a British officer or as an Indian officer. They held equal status and must be referred to as KCOs (to distinguish them from VCOs).

After Colonel Tarver's action in downgrading and removing Johnson, I had a vacancy for a captain. Drurie-Brewer was acting temporarily as second-in-command and I wished to promote either him or Tim Eaton, both of whom were suitable. However the days of the casual promotions of a year ago had passed. When I had promoted Johnson I had been on the road between Delhi and Agra and I had been ordered to promote immediately any officer I wished. Now that was not possible; there was a promotion block. This block had arisen partly because, while the younger officers had joined up before the older men and so had the longer service, yet the older men — I mean those between 25 and 30 — seemed the logical ones to promote. One of the things that is now perhaps forgotten about the war was remarked upon recently by Enoch Powell:

"We expected to carry on where we left off in 1918. That was when an infantry officers' expectation of life was only three weeks."

This had meant that in 1939 good officers and men for the infantry had not been easy to find. It was not until July 1940 that the English were really ready to fight. Few men were 'raring to go' in 1939 but they were by late 1940, and also by that time it was clear that it was not going to be a trench war with all its horrors.

Colonel Singh knew both Tim and Drurie and said that as neither of them had passed the Urdu exam, he was not prepared to confirm either of them as captain. If either passed the exam within three months he would promote him; if they both failed to do so he must promote from outside.

With Drurie as second-in-command I saw a great deal more of him. His clerical manners grew even more solemn.

"My dear Major," he would say, putting his fingers together as though in prayer, "as the evening shadows fall, perhaps you and I deserve a drink, taken of course as everything else in life, in moderation."

When Drurie-Brewer had had his drink or two, naturally in moderation, he liked to discuss his conquests. The rule about not talking about girls in the mess only applies when you are in a station where there are girls who everybody knows. It certainly did not apply to girl-starved officers out in the jungle. We were willing listeners as Drurie was the only one of us who really had had much experience. As he was rather a snob, his amours, which were never too explicit, would end something like this:

"So when she asked me to meet her that evening behind the ruined temple I could hardly refuse. After all, she was the Major's wife."

"Naturally I accepted the invitation for a breakfast picnic up in the hills. When I rode up I found she had arranged everything. The fire was burning, breakfast was cooking and there were blankets to lie on. She was, of course, the Brigadier's daughter."

I listened spellbound. The girls I had known in Delhi and Simla had never been so easy, in fact, they hadn't been easy at all.

A year before the Army had been searching desperately for people to promote. Now they knew who they wished to promote but there were no vacancies. Any mistake and one was out and down in rank. Of the twelve GPT companies in the area, only two of the original COs were now left. The other majors had vanished either through sickness or demotion: they went very quickly and one never heard the reason for their going. I began to feel like one of the ten green bottles sitting on the wall.

When one was depressed one's mosquito net at night was a great source of comfort. Outside let the mosquitoes buzz, let the snakes and centipedes crawl, let the bats swirl; inside, with an inspection light run off a battery by which to read, all was secure and Evelyn Waugh's books could be read for the third time with pleasure. A further point was that when a mosquito landed on the outside of the net, it presented a perfect view of how it sat. This was very important as all malaria mosquitoes are anopheles and all the varied types of anopheles sit with their bottoms higher than their heads, that is, they slope up from head to tail, while all other mosquitoes slope the other way, their heads being higher than their bottoms.

About this time I met an old Etonian of my own age who told me that Basil Fisher, whom I had known well at my preparatory school, had been killed in the Battle of Britain. He had been captain of cricket at Eton and I had kept up with him all my school days while I was at Repton.

Basil's death made me wonder why I myself was in the relative safety of a Transport Company. I had not enlisted or applied for the RIASC but, having enlisted in the ranks of the Royal Engineers, had been posted away as I had no engineering qualifications suitable for a commission. While in GHQ Delhi I never received any criticism. Even when dining at the Commander-in-Chief's house with Lady Wavell, there was no flicker of disapproval in the General's face when he heard that I was not in a fighting formation. Now, however, in 1943 I began to be conscious of the fact that I should be in something more active; perhaps this was due to my constant contacts with 17 Division who were so proud of themselves.

However, since the war I have been astonished at the number of officers of fighting units who never saw a shot fired in anger. One man having fought bravely but without much enthusiasm, both up and down Burma, returned to his depot five years later to find some officers still there. They had never moved out of the depot; this was not uncommon.

Chapter 5
GRINDING DISCIPLINE

In a letter to my father I wrote, 'It is extraordinary the extra fillip that the threat of a Colonel's inspection gives the unit. Every platoon guard is well turned out, every cookhouse clean, every latrine covered. These deep trench latrines are bamboo palaces. The water table here is at 18 inches and to get a 6-foot drop, one has to build up mud walls of over 5 feet and on top of that, because of the rain, put on a bamboo hut and roof. This gives a total height of 12 feet. If the drop is not fully 6 feet, flies breed in their millions; you can then see the surface alive with the shimmering movement of larvae; it is unforgettable.'

With dysentry rife every officer of that force of 100,000 men then in Imphal must, that monsoon, have peered into latrine after latrine. Colonels and medical officers homed in onto them first and no wonder with the threat of cholera always with us. The Indian troops thought the whole thing quite absurd and one of the company songs roughly translated ran, 'Every officer sahib enjoys looking at shit.'

About this time Tim, who was still ill from malaria, was sent by me on long study leave back to the great house in Madras where his mother and stepfather lived in colonial splendour with twenty servants. He had instructions to pass his Urdu exam at all costs. He did not succeed in doing so. On his way back he put in some time investigating the drink situation in Calcutta. He made a direct contract with a rum factory to supply us rum at wholesale prices by the barrel free of duty. The only problem was we had to detail someone returning from leave to fetch it. We were now permitted to send quite a number of our men on leave each week, and we always took up our full quota. Somewhat to my surprise practically all the men came back, but hardly any of them brought back their blankets. These they left with their families and then happily accepted the official fine, which must have been pitched too low.

Both my brother and brother-in-law were now in India and we arranged to take leave together and meet in Darjeeling. There we easily got rooms in the Planters' Club because as Drurie had said, all the planters were away planting. The club could not have been more comfortable. I arrived last of the three and was met by my brother at the station, which was the terminus of the small hill railway. I was carrying nothing when I met him and he asked me where my suitcase was. I turned round and pointed to where my batman was unloading a table, a chair, a camp bed, a roll of bedding, a picnic basket, a hurricane light and a suitcase. Officers of the Indian Army in those days always travelled with a servant and camp equipment. At the hill station snow lay on the ground and this fascinated my orderly, who had never seen it before. We hired hill ponies and rode and walked in the pine-clad hills. There was always the sound of running water, the delicious smell of woodsmoke and the snow-capped mountains in the distance. Afterwards we would return to the excellent library and first class food and services of the Club. It was India at its best. My brother-in-law, an engineer, had arrived first and made sure of our comfort. Engineers are like that.

I came back from leave far less short-tempered and found that in my absence the company was running perfectly well under Drurie-Brewer. I was able to leave him at it and with each platoon officer go through the NCOs with a toothcomb. We made a number of promotions and demotions. I wrote to my father, 'A full Naik (Corporal) who can run a convoy and may command 15 men on secondment on his own, only earns nine rupees a month more than a Sepoy; that is quite ridiculous.' About then, Havildar Clerk Kuttanpan Nair, while rootling through regulations at my request, discovered that we were entitled to award specialist pay to some 30 NCOs and this I did. It was a great fillip to the company. I also found to my dismay that while I was away a 5-ounce bar of gold, which I had bought in Delhi, had been stolen from my suitcase. I was more or less convinced that it had been taken by a young sepoy, a small nervous man with blue eyes, which are unusual in India. He worked in the officers' mess and now looked even more anxious. He was going on leave shortly and I was sure that my small gold bar (worth by present values over £1,000) was going to be in the leave lorry which would drive them down to Dimapur. I considered having a thorough search made but it seemed such an undignified start to their leave for all the other men who would have had to be searched too. In an odd way now it gives me pleasure to think of that young sepoy slipping his fingers into a narrow slit in the suitcase and coming out with the prize of all prizes, completely unexpected, a bar of gold capable of buying a field, ten buffaloes, and perhaps a dowry for his sister. It was worth twenty years' pay.

With all the officers going on leave, it now became James Hamilton's turn and off he went to a hill station in the Nilgris. Shortly after he got back he came very shamefacedly to see me.

"I have got syphilis," he said.

"That's a damn silly thing to have done; why weren't you more careful?"

"I thought it would be all right because she was a major's wife. Who can you trust if not a major's wife?" He felt very hard done by.

That major's wife must have caused havoc in the army among the young officers on leave. Hamilton, with a misguided sense of honour, would not give me her name, but she should have been reported and dealt with.

As Hamilton wished to become a doctor, before going on leave he had spent much of his spare time at the big General Hospital near Imphal. Here he had been quite a favourite with the nurses and it was therefore very embarrassing for him when he turned up there in the VD ward. It was an offence to catch VD and as he got on badly with both Tim and Drurie he was not an officer I particularly wished to keep, so I was glad to be able to use the excuse to post him back to India. I gave him a reasonable report because he had somewhere the makings of a good officer, but not under me.

All this time we were working over a very wide area. My policy of handing over the allocation of daily work tasks to platoon officers had made our company a favourite with the Engineers. Each platoon officer could, right up to the last moment, adjust the orders as to where his lorries would report. This was not the general policy of other companies as most issued their daily orders only through their own headquarters.

One forward platoon was now up the mountain beyond Palel and came in daily contact with John Henslow who was in 59

Indian Field Company. We supplied his lorries but his men were drawn from a Bengali Pioneer battalion; this was commanded, because of its size, by a Lt.-Col. who outranked the senior local engineer, who could not therefore insist on his orders being carried out. This particular Lt.-Col. regarded his 1,000 men as his personal retinue and would only allow the engineers 200 men for the road while the other 800 men were busy building extraordinary palaces of bamboo for themselves and their officers. In the main palace bedroom the Lt.-Colonel's bed and that of his young orderly stood side by side.

"My dear," he would tell anyone who would listen, "the young boys I have saved from corruption in Calcutta. They were all too, too grateful and the Bishop of Calcutta so appreciates my work. I am a very good influence on the young." He would bring out snapshots of the young boys he had influenced.

The quartermaster of this fantastic company was an Armenian who, instead of issuing the rations of tinned fruit to his men, had built himself a hut of packing cases of figs, peaches and pears. He counted them regularly. Here we had another Pooh Bear. Finally, the second in command was a German who was a regulations buff. No one got any of his men without filling in a complicated form in triplicate, which had to be approved by the signature of his commanding officer. This expensive battalion was practically useless to the Engineers and had a very bad effect on the maintenance of the road.

War is a matter of a small amount of fierce fighting and a great deal of supply logistics. Some good young infantry officers might at times have been better employed in getting the best out of their support companies but there was little liaison. It was sad to see the mess the Tamu road got into, and in the worst of the next monsoon some of 23 Division had to withdraw as they could not be supplied down the rutted muddy track it had become.

This happened when I had a platoon stationed at Palel. It was commanded by Rolfe and was now thoroughly efficient. We had an urgent order to send food up the Tamu road to 23 Division. The road was now as bad as the Tiddim Track had been at its worst. The divisional transport had only to get supplies forward thirty-five miles but, while they had got the ammunition and petrol up, food had virtually run out. I knew the road so I told Gordon to take seven days' rations for the total journey of seventy miles. He set out with twenty-five lorries; it took him six days averaging 6 miles a day to reach the Division: that is well under one mile an hour. Round every corner of that twisting road there was another lorry bogged down. Each time the sandbags, the shovels, the planks and the tow ropes had to be used again. He reached the Divisional rear troops and passed through them. Eventually a Major General, the Divisional commander himself, stopped him.

"How the hell did you get those lorries through? I thought we'd have to use mules. Don't go any further, the Japs are four hundred yards ahead."

The lorries were unloaded quickly enough with volunteers but there was no turning point. It took him a day to turn all the lorries and get them free to start back. By then he had run out of rations and had to draw fresh ones from the Division. Eleven days after he started he arrived back exhausted from the journey of seventy miles. It was this type of experience which led the army to rely more and more on air drops.

I had a formal visit from the local Manipuri Headman, who asked me and Drurie-Brewer to come to the dance of Sri Krishna, which was being held some 300 yards away.

The dance location was impressive: a large, roofed and raised platform, open all round, had been brightly lit by many pressure lamps. These lamps were rare in the area and their number showed the importance of the ceremony. There was an orchestra of drums and other instruments, all the players of which were dressed in snow-white dhotis and each wore a pugri, far larger than any I had seen before, and snow white. Some of the players were distinguished by a slash of red cloth worn from the shoulder in a way similar to the Garter. There was a supporting cast of about 15 children, but the main actor was a small boy aged ten, dressed in red, yellow, and tinsel. He had to dance for some six hours on end and was rarely off the stage. Beside the stage sat a prompter and a teacher to whom he looked at intervals for support. This dance is the most sacred that the Manipuris have and the honour of dancing it can only come once in a lifetime to a child of a rich and high caste family. The boy's family had to pay for all the orchestra's expenses and for the food and drink for the audience. As we did not understand the words or the story, after four hours our good manners faltered and at 2 o'clock in the morning, on the plea of early duty, we gave our thanks and apologies to the Headman and withdrew.

The Manipuris with their soft dark faces always looked clean and, unlike the hill tribes, they were always washing either their clothes or themselves. As they washed, the young girls would glance up from under their fringes, giggle and glance away. In the evening they wore red hibiscus or the sweet-smelling frangipani tucked behind their ears. Their lustrous hair fell heavy and sleek over their bare smooth shoulders, their saris were wrapped tight above their breasts and below their arms — most seductive.

Shortly after this I was offered a move in the same rank, back to India to a training wing, but I was now so involved with the company that I asked for the posting to be withdrawn, which it was. It was probably a mistake to get so tied up mentally with the company but I had started it from scratch and could not bear to leave it.

On the front we had never up to then had an inspection by a Major General. Now we had one and came out of it very well.

In July 1943 a very serious famine started in Bengal and men and officers coming back from leave reported that there were dead bodies all over Howrah station and on the streets of Calcutta. Those streets and the station were, for many thousands of families, their only homes and now they were starving to death where they slept. The Viceroy, at the request of Wavell as Commander-in-Chief, unexpectedly clamped down emergency powers against hoarding. On searching the port warehouses it was found that there were large stocks of rice there which were being stored by merchants in the hopes of a further rise in price. A fair price was fixed and within a week the famine was over and there were no more problems. It was a dramatic intervention.

Drurie-Brewer was down in Calcutta at the time and said the food at Firpos (the best restaurant) at first seemed good. However, when he ordered a chicken curry, he looked at it and moved the bones about.

"Khidmagar (waiter)," he said, "this chicken is rabbit."

"No, no, I assure you, sahib, is very best pussy cat."

About this time we lost our friendly Colonel, 'Biscuit' Singh, who was posted back to India for promotion. Instead I had an Indian Colonel who came and stayed with me for three days. All the colonels would stay with us — most unnecessary. He was an ambitious regular and a real demon for efficiency. He had a list of two hundred questions to which I had to give answers. He was the only annoying Indian Officer I met. Under him we were forever carrying out fire drills, checking air pressures, checking batteries, checking food consumption, carrying out kit inspections, etc., etc. We doubted if, when the impending battles came, this training would be much use. It drove Tim crazy with irritation.

"That bloody man wouldn't have lasted a day in the old days (a year before). Two or three bouts of malaria and he'd have been off back to India."

This particular Colonel caught us out on something. I can't remember exactly what it was, but it was connected with the quartermaster's accounting system and the Colonel slammed into me personally.

As he slated me, I stood rigidly to attention using that old army defence, 'do not make excuses'. He should not, however, have disciplined me in front of several of my own NCOs. I think he enjoyed, as an Indian, ticking off an Englishman in front of Indians. I never met a situation like this again, and this was the only Indian KCO from whom I did not get an absolutely fair deal. When the battle for Imphal started a few months later, it was this same Colonel who was the senior officer in charge of the large depot at Milestone 109 on the Tiddim Track. When the Japanese attack came in, he made no defence but panicked and, with his staff, took to the hills. He was not Court Martialled but lost his command and was flown out shortly afterwards.

My workshop under Conductor Snowden was working very well, and now out of the blue we had a Workshops Officer appointed to us. His name was Dobbs (or was it Dibbs?) and he was another regulation buff, with a social inferiority complex which was only too justified. Platoon officers started complaining that they could not get any spare parts out of the workshop. The workshop stores clerk had instructions from Dibbs not to issue spares without proper vouchers and, as most of the best NCOs could not write in Roman script, they were unable to get any spares. Dibbs was bringing my lorries to a halt.

I knew there were other GPT companies who did not have good warrant officers like Snowden and were wanting workshop officers, so on the 'old boy network' I was able to get him moved on within a couple of weeks. Meanwhile the workshop spares lorry had at long last arrived loaded with a quite incredible number of unwanted spares and missing, of course, the clutch plates and the petrol washers which we really needed.

When Dobbs learned of his posting he put it down, quite rightly, to my influence and he therefore plotted a little Dobbish type of revenge. He personally checked and counted every screw, bolt and washer in the spares lorry. These must have amounted to several thousand and as we were in the middle of the rainy season, with its great humidity, it must have been a most unpleasant job inside the metal body of the lorry. Armed at last with twenty-eight pages detailing the spares, he called in formally to see me.

"I am not prepared, sir," he said, fixing me with an aggressive glare, "to hand the spares over to anyone but yourself. Snowden is not an officer and as I am senior in rank to all your other officers, I must insist that you take these stores on your personal charge. I must officially inform you, sir, that it is your duty, as laid down in para 482 (sub-para c) of the regulations on stores, to check all the items and sign for them."

"Tell me, Captain Dibbs," I said (with a slight emphasis on the Captain, which I would not normally have used), "have you yourself personally checked all these items, and are they in order?"

"Yes, sir," he replied, "I have checked each item and I can vouch for them being correct. As you see I have myself signed every one of these twenty-eight sheets."

"In that case Dobbs," (or was it Dibbs?) I said, "as I know I can trust you, I will now give you clearance on all your stores and take them on my personal charge."

Sitting in the cool of the thatched office I signed all twenty-eight sheets in duplicate, handed him the top copy and arranged for my station wagon to take him to his new posting. He was another one of those who were convinced there would be a great accounting after the war. I never of course had any comeback on this and throughout the war I cheerfully signed any documents I considered necessary for my unit.

We now received a very odd order to grow our own vegetables and with it came dozens of packets of seed. The order was passed to all units and some hundreds of acres were planted up. Nothing makes one more reluctant to move than vegetables almost at the picking stage. Our army newspaper *SEAC* (of which I still have a copy) told us that Major-General 'Alf' Snelling had planned the planting of 18,000 acres of vegetable gardens in 14 Army area. Only a man with a name like Alf could have thought up something quite so ridiculous.* Why are generals referred to in the press by their Christian names? During the war I never heard General Slim called Bill or indeed any other general by a Christian name or nickname. No one called them anything as one rarely saw or heard of them.

Our vegetable garden was quite interesting as all the seeds grew like mad in that soil and heat. As we were always being moved before they were ready, the only thing we ever actually ate were radishes. It all seemed rather pointless but probably the Manipuris or the goats ate them.

While we were growing vegetables Snowden and Sgt. Goodbury had taken to keeping ducks. This they did with great success and were soon selling eggs to all the officers' messes in the area. Ducks are quite attractive birds to watch, but they do seem to have an energetic sex life.

---

*I have just had a letter saying that Snelling was a first class officer and good to work under. General Slim had a very high opinion of him.

Chapter 6

COBRAS

At the time the army was combing through all VCOs in order to find those suitable to promote to KCOs. Since my two best VCOs, as soon as I had recommended them for King's Commissions, had been killed by lorries overturning on top of them, I had no one left who I considered good enough. Also, after the two deaths I felt a sense of superstition in recommending anyone. Jemadar Rudolf was of course absolutely certain that he was suitable and I was really pestered by him. His application for a King's Commission started (I kept the file):

> 'My heart burns with high aspirations and the blood of fidelity runs in my veins. It is the policy of the benign government to encourage the youths of noble families and to kindle in their hearts more dauntlessness. . ."

By this time I, for my part, was sure that I had here a real top rank rogue and at two official interviews he sought with me I refused to put forward his name. VCOs, being commissioned direct by the Viceroy, had very strong rights indeed, and he asked for a formal interview with my Lt.-Colonel, the new one. He impressed the Colonel very much and I was advised, no, instructed, to forward his name for a King's Commission. This, to the annoyance of the Colonel, I refused to do. Jemadar Rudolf was therefore sent off by the Colonel out of the immediate area for a four-week stay with another GPT company. He behaved in an exemplary way and came back with a glowing report. However, he could not get his King's Commission without my signature as his Commanding Officer and this I still refused to give. The Colonel was most upset but I stuck to my guns because I knew that, although likeable and in some ways very efficient, Rudolf was a dangerous man and completely without scruples. Under pressure, however, I agreed that if he got another good report from another company, I would sign.

Rudolf was then sent off for a further period of testing to a Reinforcement Camp in India. Six weeks later he returned as smart, bright and friendly as ever and informed me cheerfully that a strong recommendation for promotion was on its way. I asked him how he was so sure.

"Well, Sahib," he said, "Captain Sahib at the camp used to keep all the men's rum in his tent just like Eaton Sahib does." (That was a covert threat.) "His orderly came and told me this, Sahib, so I carried out faithfully my duty to the Army and the King." (He never used the term King Emperor, which was the polite usage by VCOs.) "I collected all VCOs in camp and took them by back way along to Captain Sahib's tent; here I showed large stocks illegal rum. Many of them signed paper to say they had seen rum, and all most iniquitous and bad behaviour on part of King's Officer."

"What happened then Jemadar Sahib?" I asked.

"I did nothing, Sahib, but let Captain Sahib's clerk know what I had seen. Soon Captain Sahib come to me and say, 'For God's sake, Jemadar Sahib, I am officer and you are my esteemed brother officer. Please to keep silent and I will quickly get you King's Commission. We must stand shoulder to shoulder.'" He paused, perhaps to emphasise to me that I too should stand shoulder to shoulder with him.

"Go on, Jemadar Sahib," I said, intrigued by the story. He was never a bore. "What happened next?"

"Nothing, Sahib, no action by Captain Sahib, so five days later I demand interview with Colonel Sahib, very senior officer, but he told that Captain Sahib did not give recommendation for King's Commission. I therefore in duty bound told Colonel Sahib all the truth. Also I tell him I had big friends in GHQ Delhi and I would make grand prestigious row about his men not getting their rum, but to help him I would forgive all if he get me in quick time King's Commission, which was proper due to me."

I awaited with interest the arrival of the Colonel's letter. It was very short:

'I am unable to recommend Jemadar Rudolf for a King's Commission.'

So here he was back on my hands again. The saga of Jemadar Rudolf was intriguing the whole unit and Subadhar Koshy, now the Indian Adjutant, said that there was a general opinion that I would have to give in. Later in the week however he reported that he had some good evidence that Jemadar Rudolf had been selling batteries to Manipuris. Batteries were like gold dust and I appointed Drurie-Brewer to take a summary of evidence with a view to a Court Martial. This summary uncovered good evidence but as Rudolf was a VCO the Court Martial would have to be carried out by a higher formation than our company. It was arranged therefore for Drurie-Brewer and me to take Jemadar Rudolf up on a charge to the Colonel the following week.

The morning that the interview was due, I went to my lavatory which was a wooden thunder box. I lifted the lid and out came a cobra's head. Startled, I dropped the lid and went to breakfast where I found Drurie-Brewer already there. On seeing me he said, "David, the most amazing thing. There's a cobra in my thunder box." I told him about my cobra.

We could prove nothing but, looking back, I am astonished how coolly we both took the incident. Murder by snake bite is not unknown in India but normally it is by krait, a much smaller snake and easier to catch and handle.

I called the mess Naik. "Both Lieutenant Sahib and I have cobras in our thunder boxes. Please inform Subadhar Koshy and ask him to have them removed."

"At once, Sahib," said the Naik, showing no surprise. India was like that — you could give any order and it would be carried out or at least they would try to carry it out.

Half an hour later the duty Havildar reported, "Subadhar Koshy asks where you and Lieutenant sahib want the cobras put."

Drurie glanced at me. "Tell the subadhar sahib to kill them."

The havildar hesitated. "Sahib," he said, "in my place, if you kill cobra, cobra's mate get much cross and waits by body to kill man."

This was one of those problems to which I had no certain answer.

"Tell Subadhar sahib to do what he thinks best," I said, opting out. I believe the cobras were handed over to the snake charmer from whom I suspect they had first come. A good Indian Adjutant like Koshy was invaluable. The British army had adjutants, normally captains, and regimental sergeant-majors. An Indian adjutant combined the positions of both and ranked mid-way between them.

We later found that the papers for the Court Martial had disappeared from Drurie's tent and we had to cancel the interview with the Colonel.

I now began to sleep with my tent carefully guarded. As Jemadar Rudolf had already made a report to me against one of my officers about homosexuality, I chose a particularly ugly sepoy to sleep just inside the entrance. Things had now reached an impasse. As the vital evidence had disappeared I could not get Rudolf Court Martialled. I could not get him posted as every unit in the area knew about him, and was watching the outcome with interest. No one would accept him. My very quiet servant Kesavan Nair was obviously aware of the problem, and came into my tent one morning on soundless bare feet.

"Sahib," he said, "all the men saying Jemadar Rudolf causing much trouble."

"That is true talk, Kesavan Nair," I replied, "but it is dangerous talk."

"Sahib, you are my man bap (mother/father), all my heart is with you. I kill Jemadar sahib at night, very easy. Everyone then happy. You give order, I kill him and tell no one. You know nothing of this talk and all is good."

I was almost tempted to accept his offer.

"Thankful I am to thee, Kesavan Nair, your talk comes from a brave heart, but this is order, absolute strict order, do not kill Jemadar sahib."

Now unexpectedly I heard from Havildar Clerk Kutappan Nair that a Manipuri had bought an army tarpaulin from the Jemadar and as it was in bad condition the Manipuri had asked for an interview with me to get his money back. This was a godsend, but I did not consider the evidence would get Rudolf anything more than a formal reprimand, so I therefore turned to Tim for help.

Tim invited Jemadar Rudolf in for a drink and then with his remarkable ability for emphasising the depressing side of any situation, he dwelt on the horrors of compulsory discharge with a bad character from the Army. "Of course," he said, "there is another way. A VCO is free to resign with an honourable discharge."

Next day Jimmy James, who had recently been sent to us as a captain (both Tim and Drurie had again failed their Urdu exams), got Rudolf's formal resignation in writing. The next step was my counter signature and at the same time I had to certify that no pressure had been brought to bear upon Rudolf to get him to resign. This I gladly did. Any officer worth his salt should be prepared to bend the truth in the general interests of the army. I signed and sent the paper up the long chain to the Viceroy's office. Now that he was going I felt quite friendly to this amusing and enterprising man.

"I hope you will be very happy in your new life, Jemadar Sahib," I said.

"I intend to set up prestigious company to supply Army with much food," he replied. "Please to give me high recommendation to senior officers in Delhi."

With a sigh of relief I sent him on indefinite leave and promised him a clean discharge when the acceptance of his resignation came through.

A fortnight passed in comparative peace and then a barrage of telegrams arrived. Jemadar Rudolf had wired GHQ India, 14th Army, 4 Corps, the Sub-Area and myself, withdrawing his resignation. I opened this telegram as I was sitting at lunch in my chair at the head of the table and to the astonishment of the officers there, I went straight to sleep as I sat. It must have been a defence mechanism and was quite a useful one.

We were back to square one and then, out of the blue, fortune played into my hands. There was some mix-up in Rudolf's bank account in Delhi, and they wired him to inform him of the amount that he had banked in Imphal in the last three months and asked for instructions. The amount banked was over three times his pay and this open telegram landed on my desk.

Jemadar Rudolf arrived back with a great flourish, friendly as a St Bernard dog, and as well turned out as ever. His King's Commission was now a certainty he told me. I pushed his post with the open telegram on the top across to him.

"You seem to be a rich man," I remarked, "with a very big income."

Jimmy James came in by arrangement, greeted him in a friendly manner and took him away for a drink. After a discussion about bank accounts Jemadar Rudolf called in again at my office and without a trace of shame said he had thought it over and perhaps after all he could make a better career outside the Army. He asked if he could send off telegrams cancelling the cancellation of his resignation. I felt so relieved at the outcome that the night before he left we gave him a small goodbye party.

The day after, a Manipuri was brought to me under arrest. He had been caught driving away one of our lorries. He was most indignant at being stopped and showed me a receipt for 2,000 rupees from Jemadar Rudolf for the sale of the lorry to him. The story does not end there: Rudolf surfaced again in 1944 in Delhi.

In the middle of 1943 most of the engineering units working on the roads and the airfields were put under command of Brigadier Westropp DSO, MC, who had his Headquarters (GREF) at the American Baptist Mission Leper Colony at Kangpokpi (the place of the mosquito bite). This was near the control post at Milestone 105 where in late 1942 the three British Military Police soldiers had died one after another of cerebral malaria. It killed each of them only three days after the first fever; over a period of two weeks they had all died. The post to me was a place of ill omen and it was also here that the Japanese were to cut the road in 1944 and to kill everyone in the new police post.

Westropp was taciturn, thin-faced, bad-tempered, and good at his job. He was very dictatorial. Later it was his idea to mark the danger spots on the road with a warning skull and crossbones. These posts however were frequently defaced by the local tribesmen, who carved parts of them into phallic symbols.

Before the road was cut at Milestone 105 by the Japanese in 1944, Ben Bazeley, one of Westropp's officers, reported that some very odd new buildings were being put up by the Kukis, who were as anti-British as the Nagas were pro-British. Later these buildings and the mission were used by the Japanese 15 Division as a base for its attack on Imphal. They may have ferried in supplies earlier.

Gordon Rolfe had his 21st birthday on the 4th October 1943, and we had the workshop staff along to dinner. The workshop duck-breeding enterprise was flourishing, and they gave us three of their ducks and came along to eat them. Everyone always drank far too much at these affairs, and one of the odd things was that there was almost always someone asleep in the corner. I record it as a fact — whether it had something to do with the height I don't know.

We had some odd speeches. After another lot of those bloody radishes which were the sole result of the 4 Corps gardening drive, Drurie gave the toast.

"I give you the toast 'Radishes and the Soya Link'. We of 4 Corps owe a great debt to that distinguished General Alf Snelling. He is the man who saw clearly that the army needed to be fitter and leaner. We are leaner and fitter soldiers because Alf has cut out meat and potatoes and given us radishes and the soya link — the only sausage in the world which is quite uneatable."

It was true the army was awash with radishes and tins of soya link sausages.* Taste soya link sausages once, they were tolerable, twice and you just got them down, three times and one could never touch them again. The tins were used as bricks for building walls and as stones for filling potholes. They now lie all over the valleys and mountains of Manipur. What wretched English officer was conned into ordering them from America? To the best of my belief American troops did not have them.

All young male parties tend to be drunken and rowdy. I still carry on the palm of my left hand a black soot mark where I cut my hand trying to roll a bath water barrel down a hill.

Near our mess, fruit bats the size of small chickens hung during the day from large mango and karnikar trees. The karnikar has large blossoms which open at night time and fall by dawn. With a 303 rifle I was now shooting these bats regularly for dinner and as they are vegetarian their flesh was not unlike chicken. They did not look too good on the table as their legs stuck up 12 inches above the carcass.

We seemed to have a lot of parties because a few days later on 17th October, it was Tim's birthday. About 11 o'clock we missed him. I went out to see the duty Havildar.

"Eaton Sahib," he said, "is sitting in that slit trench throwing stones at the guard."

I went over with the Havildar and spoke to Tim. I asked him if he was enjoying himself in that trench.

"No," he replied, "I am doing my duty. Your HQ guards are

---

*I have heard recently from Major C.R. Jenkinson who, while in Calcutta, handled the supply of Lease-Lend soya link sausages from America. He says, 'It was a nightmare. No one would eat them.' In the end the Americans took back 2,000 tons and sent them to the Chinese Army. What a waste of transport space by sea, land and air as the sausages were shuttled about the world.

so slack that I feel I have to teach them to keep alert at all times."

I thought for a moment and then spoke with the guard commander and the duty Havildar. "It is the day of birth for Eaton Sahib," I explained, "and in Vilayat (England) we allow special privileges for this special Burra Din (big day)."

The Havildar was most amused. "I will watch over the Sahib," he said, "and see he gets to tent in good way."

Christmas was coming up fast and I see we each had four free letter forms issued to us. Evidently we must have been paying for our other letters which up till then had been photographed and shrunk and then enlarged again in England. Now, following the victory at Alamein, planes were able to fly direct to England and my letters on my father's file are again proper airmail ones similar to those we use today.

In a mixed religious unit, confusion was caused by so many feast days. Apart from Christmas and Easter, we recognized Devali, the Hindu Festival of Light, and also a Malayali one called Onam. Christmas was made an official holiday and we invited all the VCOs and Havildars in for drinks before lunch. This amounted to about thirty and we had various dishes marked Hindu and Christian. Christians will happily eat Hindu food, so we had more of those, but marking the dishes convinced the Hindus that we had been careful of their religious requirements, which we had. Drinks were a problem because, as soon as you filled a Havildar's glass, he drank it at once; we had to ask them to slow down and sip drinks in the English fashion. Havildar Paranjpe had stationed himself beside a Mohammedan teetotaller (not all of them were) and was drinking two to everyone else's one. There were several Indian Missionary Christians present and to my amazement, at the end after a little whispering together, they struck up 'Auld Lang Syne'. The evening ended with Sgt. Goodbury and Paddy Hamill both being thrown into the nearby tank, a big square pond used by the Manipuris for washing and drinking. Neither of them were amused.

The parties we had — looking back on it — were really very odd. There were, of course, few girls in the area. Everybody was young and at that time thoroughly healthy because it was the cold weather season. As there were no fields larger than a tenth of an acre there were virtually no games playable and there was a great deal of pent-up energy. Heavy drinking leaves you the next morning with a hangover, but also seems to relieve general tension. It worked so well with the British that, after a discussion with the Indian adjutant, I decided to let the men have a really drunken party. We could always get hold of plenty of rum, although we now had to buy it, ex bond, in twenty-six gallon casks (half a hogshead). The cost worked out at about one shilling a bottle. The plan for the day was made with care, and with the agreement of the engineering units for whom we worked. All the guards were non-drinkers and we also had on duty a VCO and Havildar who did not drink; all King's Officers were asked to drink lightly. The men then had a feast with extra goats killed, extra purchases of vegetables and also, very important, popadums bought with the company funds. I was astonished that none of my men could cook popadums. Always on feast days a purchase of popadums was at the top of the list of requirements. The day went very well and we repeated it afterwards on a number of occasions.

I sent my father a copy of the typed programme for New Year's Eve and looking at it now I find it rather sad. It shows a very inward-looking group of men trying hard to provide their own amusements. For Christmas 1945 in Singapore we had no need of such laboured jokes, we had girls instead.

CONFIDENTIAL No. 309 Ind. GPT Company
Dated 27-12-43

All Officers
309 Ind. GPT Coy., and Workshop Section.

SUBJECT: DINNER — NEW YEARS EVE

You and your ducks are invited to dinner in the Officers mess.
(a) TRANSPORT The breakdown lorry will report at 19.00 hours to tow you round in a Goodbury 3rd line wreck.
(b) FOOD All ducks in Workshop will parade at 08.00 hours on 30-12-43 and will be marched round by Hav. Paranjpe (Sober).
(c) DRINK Drink is being kindly supplied by Capt. James and Lt. Drurie-Brewer. These officers are not aware of this measure but we feel sure they will be happy to have us drink their December rations while they are away.

(d) A programme is attached.

>D. R. Atkins
>MAJOR
>OC 309 Ind. GPT Company

Copy to:

Capt. Hamill (please bring round spare Sub Area ducks).

Capt. James/Lt. Drurie-Brewer (The cost of your December ration is Rs. 44/-. Please send cheques with your Christmas cards).

Miss Fleurette Pelly/Miss Christine Rosslyn (If possible please give Capt. Hamill the slip and report here for dinner direct).

(The girls didn't arrive. The Brigadier stole them for his own party.)

PROGRAMME

1. 'Flit Gun Dance' by Sgt. Goodbury.
2. 'Oh Don't Take my Workshop Away' sung by Sub-Conductor Snowden.
3. OC will climb the main tent pole.
4. Lt. Eaton will start a free fight.
5. Sgt. Goodbury will fall asleep as usual.
6. Capt. Hamill will lecture on 'Staff Appointments'.
7. Lt. Eaton will start a free fight.
8. Sgt. Minnit will write another letter home.
9. The OC will make a few remarks on Fords. This item will be deleted if ladies are present.
10. It is regretted Lt. Drurie-Brewer will not be here to tell his JOKE.
11. Lt. Rolfe will give excerpts from Capt. James and Lt. Drurie-Brewer's backchat act 'How 48 Brigade blew up the Sittang Bridge behind Lt. Drurie-Brewer and the ICI'.
12. Company song 'Over the Khud' will be sung by whole party. This will be sung driving up track in 15-cwts. Lt. Eaton will not drive.

The songs that we sung in these parties were rarely if ever sentimental. The most interesting one was the Alphabet Song with the chorus:
>'Roly, poly, gammon and spinach,
>Hey ho sang Sir Anthony Roly.'

It must have dated back to the Wars of the Roses.

'Bless 'em all' and 'The Quartermaster's Stores' were sung in Training Camps and by ENSA (entertainment groups), but not up at the front. 'Run Rabbit, Run' and 'We're Going to Hang out the Washing on the Siegfried Line' were not genuine army songs, but had been produced to order for the media. They died a shameful death after Dunkirk.

The Indian songs were more sentimental than ours, but some had the same sex content, such as 'Master Jawani', a line of which was, 'Quickly, quickly, little master soldier, quickly please.'

The Sikhs were supposed to have some homosexual marching songs; one frequently quoted was:

> There is a boy living over the river,
> Whose bottom is smooth as a peach,
> But alas the river is deep,
> And no one has taught me to swim.'

The Sikh boy training battalions were reported to be surrounded by tall barbed wire. A friend told me that when he had a Sikh Company attached, the British officer in charge was found knifed. As he knew nothing of Indian troops he consulted an Indian Army Colonel who knew Sikhs.

"Discuss it with your holy man," he was told.

He sent for his holy man who turned out to be one of his ordinary sepoys.

"The officer deserved to die," the sepoy said and then would say nothing more. The death was reported as natural causes.

The Sikhs were a mystery to the rest of the Indian army. Few British officers understood them.

"Trouble in a Sikh unit," an experienced officer told me, "starts unexpectedly with knives. Trouble in south Indian units starts with a rumble of voices and the waving of sticks — you have time to think." I found this to be true.

Indian swear words concentrated as much on the sexual parts as did the British ones but they had more variety and ingenuity. One avoided using any English swear words to one's men, but, 'Tum bloody fool hai', 'You are a bloody fool', was used by British and Indian alike and seemed to be understood throughout India and not resented. The Indian soldier knew all of the British swear words and would not tolerate being sworn at by British army soldiers. Complaints would come back quickly. While it was unsafe for an English soldier to swear at an Indian, it was quite safe for an Indian to swear in Urdu at a British soldier as the words were never understood.

That long wait of 1943, when boredom was our worst enemy, was enlivened for all of us by the knowledge that thirty miles away across the mountains was a large and extremely efficient Japanese army poised for battle. Behind us was an India which perhaps was an unknown element. In Bengal, to the rear of the army, police stations were being attacked and Indian policemen's eyes gouged out, so there was undoubtedly a fifth column behind us. British officers in the Mutiny were murdered by men in whom they had complete trust; was our faith in the Indian soldier as well founded as we felt it to be? Would a Japanese success make it possible to have a rising in India? There was also the odd fact that because of our great victories over the Italians in North Africa, there were now over 150,000 Italian prisoners of war in India. These far outnumbered the British forces and indeed there were now more Italian than British generals in the country. This was a potential danger if they should break out of their camps.

By now we had all heard each other's stories many times, and at the age of 25 very few people have had many odd experiences; the old, if the young would listen, have the good stories. Tim always provided an uncertain element because, when he had drunk too much, he wanted to fight. We always succeeded in stopping him hitting anyone who ranked higher than himself, but he really would have liked to have a go at Jimmy James. Jimmy, my Captain, had a tremendous chip on his shoulder. He had been educated in India and had never been to England. He was a good officer, hardworking and very cheerful, but touch upon his raw streak, even by talking about England, and he might go off like a squib. Because of this chip he appeared too English.

"I say Tim old man," he would brush his golden moustache up on both sides as he spoke, "this isn't good enough. Can't let the company down; your fire precautions are not up to standard, what."

"Bugger the fire precautions."

"I say, that's not cricket old man, got to play fair by the Major Sahib, what."

"Bugger the major sahib," replied Tim stamping off. He really was most difficult for Jimmy to handle and with Tim and me being old friends, it was not easy for Jimmy.

After a few months I recommended Jimmy for promotion and saw my new English Colonel about him. It would have been very easy to have sent an Indian Captain on a promotion course, but the British social lines still held. Jimmy James, although British through and through, could never then have got into the Saturday Club in Calcutta or the Gymkhana Club in Delhi.

"You do realise James is 'country bottled'," said my Colonel. "I doubt if he will pass the course."

"I think he might be given a chance, sir," I replied. "After all, he will be living in India when we have all gone home." How the word 'home' used to annoy Jimmy.

I got him onto the course but he failed, and naturally put this down to his background. He spoke English almost perfectly, certainly a lot better than many new officers.

We did not have much success with promotions. It would not be until early in 1944 that Tim at last passed his Urdu exam after about the tenth attempt, so neither Drurie nor Tim could complain at Jimmy's appointment. Snowden went off on an officer course and failed and when Jimmy James went off on his promotion course Drurie-Brewer was refused a temporary captaincy while Jimmy was away.

Chapter 7

A GIRL AND A MUTINY

I had a welcome visit from Bruce Rust. He had stayed with me in Delhi on the day the *Prince of Wales* and the *Repulse* were sunk. It was the worst day of the war for me. I was very ill indeed and the illness had not been diagnosed. A young doctor that day recognised it as jaundice, a disease which I greatly feared. Then, in a burst of unprofessional confidence, he unburdened himself.

"There's something wrong with Wavell's eye. I have just come from there and I think he will lose it. I shall be a footnote in history — the man who lost the war in the East by losing the Commander-in-Chief's only eye."

I felt this news was the final straw and too much for me to bear. Somehow it all seemed to be my fault.

Now in Imphal, eighteen months later, Bruce said, "I heard your name in Delhi the other day. Were you the cause of the surplus of Shakapara biscuits for British troops?"

I thought this was one of my mistakes which had finally been buried. The biscuit manufacturers in early 1942 were having difficulty in getting certain raw materials and had written to GHQ India asking for approval for certain changes in the content of the biscuit. The application landed up on my desk. After a couple of telephone calls I had cheerfully approved the alterations. There was a pause of about four months, then the Viceroy sent for the Commander-in-Chief, the Commander-in-Chief sent for the Quartermaster-General, the Quartermaster-General sent for the Director-General of Supplies and in the end my Colonel sent for me.

"Atkins," he had said, "I am not entitled to sign that authority, neither is the Director-General of Supplies. The Quartermaster-General could not have signed it and the Commander-in-Chief had not the authority. It was even outside the powers of the

Viceroy. Ever since the Mutiny, changes in ready-cooked food for Hindu soldiers have required the approval of the Viceroy in full Council and you, as a Captain, have given this approval on your own."

Shakapara bicuits, which were the hard tack of the army, were cooked under two religious processes with regular inspections by Hindu and Moslem holy men. It was one of these who had picked up the change in the manufacturing process which I had approved. All the biscuits made during those last months had therefore to be marked 'For the use of British troops only'. I doubt whether they ever got eaten, but they were not too bad with butter and jam, and could be crumbled down to make porridge or pudding.

The Sepoys when filling their lorries with the inefficient four gallon cans which we used, would drip petrol about. One could not get them to treat it as really valuable; after all there were always more tins at the petrol dump. At home my Father was getting only one gallon a month. My Mother was extremely ill and unable to get about except by car and my Father's petrol was carefully treasured in order to take her to church once a week. I lectured all the senior NCOs on the petrol situation — mentioning my Father — but they did not believe me. Anyone so much a 'rajah' as the Major Sahib's father could not possibly not have access to unlimited petrol. This slackness over petrol was to cause a terrible death a few weeks later.

The Engineer now running the Tiddim Track was Max Gray and when the rains ceased and the ground dried out we came out of our monsoon quarters at Imphal and went back to very much the same sites as we had occupied before. In one of the lovely glades was sited the platoon commanded by Gordon Rolfe, and Drurie-Brewer and I went up one evening to dine with him. As we got out of the car there was an explosion nearby. Naik Raphai, who should have known better, had been filling a petrol tank whilst smoking a cigarette and the can had exploded all over him. Leaving Drurie-Brewer to look after the platoon, we bundled Raphai into the back of my station wagon and, while Gordon drove, I held him struggling in my arms. He was very badly burned indeed and in considerable pain. I talked to him as we drove.

"The Doctor Sahib will help you. We will soon be there and he will give you medicine for the pain. The Company will gladly welcome you back because you are one of our good Naiks and we need you."

Somewhat to my surprise he understood what I was saying, and replied on two or three occasions, always in the same way.

"Who will come back, not Naik Raphai. Naik Raphai is dead, this naik is finished."

Those were his exact words, in Urdu of course.

There was a good Casualty Clearing Station in the jungle where a doctor treated him at once, but he died in the night. He was a Hindu so we had no trouble in giving him a proper funeral, Havildar Paranjpe officiating, and as there was firewood all around the funeral pyre was more than adequate. There is nothing worse than burning a body with too little wood. What in the world did the army in the desert do with their dead Hindus?

Another death we had about this time was a Roman Catholic sepoy — Thomas. The manual of Indian Military Law came to my aid and I found that, in the absence of a priest it was my duty, like a ship's captain, to hold the service. We did not know of the existence on the Track of a Catholic padre but to our surprise shortly before the funeral one turned up out of the blue and took over.

For the first year on the front I had lived in the tent laid down for my rank, which was known as a twelve pounder, but later I began to believe that in the Indian Army if one lived in some style, the Indian did tend to respect one more. I changed, therefore, to a larger tent. This was about 12 feet square with side walls and in it I lived in considerable comfort with a bath tent at the back. I soothed my conscience with the fact that this same tent was the entitlement of any Staff Captain and I had lived in one in Delhi exactly like it.

Now that it was planting time for rice, the tribes set fire to the hillside and chains of golden fire crept at night along the sides of the mountain. The mountain rice, which is smaller and sweeter than ordinary rice, can only be grown in one field for two years before the soil is exhausted. There is no terracing, so they then burn off another part of the hillside in order to create a new planting area. The combination of burning and the rainfall of over 200 inches a year causes tremendous erosion and villages have to move on frequently. There is a twenty-year cycle of use of the mountains and in this sparsely populated area there is deep land hunger. Language changes every forty or fifty miles and as the tribes are all headhunters each village is highly protected against attack by their neighbours. For defence reasons the villages are built on the tops of the hills and, as there is no water there, the women spend much of their lives fetching it. Water is carried in pieces of thick bamboo, five or six to a basket, each slice of bamboo being about 2 feet long and containing about three pints. The baskets hang down the women's backs and the weight is taken by carrying bands across their foreheads. Among the Nagas the head bands are brightly embroidered, very often in red and blue.

There was only one person who was really trusted by the Nagas. Twenty miles west of Imphal lived an English girl who now became a living legend. Ursula Bower had come out to India in 1937 and had been invited by a girl friend to stay in Imphal where her father was President of the Manipur State Durbar. Two lovely girls in that tiny community were a godsend and Ursula first travelled with the Government Doctor and his wife across the Ukruhl country of the Tangkhul Nagas, later to be the centre of fierce fighting, and then she and her friend were invited to join the State Engineer on a bridge inspection trip to the Tamenlong track where the Zemi Nagas lived. From there they came down the Barak river by raft to the Silchar Track. Later she travelled the mountains on her own dealing with the sick. By the time the war came she was already a Naga legend.

The stories around her grew, helped by the fact that Masang, one of the great Naga headmen, believed that Ursula was the reincarnation of the goddess Gaidiliu.

In August 1942, when it was expected by the locals that the Imphal plain would fall to the Japanese, Ursula was asked by three of the Naga tribes to take over the leadership from the British when they went.

Then, as the front stabilised, she was asked by 'V' Force to form their Watch and Ward section and was put in command of 800 square miles of mountains in the Tamenlong area. She had to do her own recruiting from Nagas. We had lost so many arms in Singapore and Burma that the army could only send her 90 long-barrelled 'Last of the Mohicans' type muzzle loaders. When she was down in Calcutta the Commanding General sent for her. As she sat in the ante-room she heard him say:

"Send in that missionary type."

She walked in as he rose to his feet.

"Good heavens, you are only a girl — a golden girl." That is what she was, fair-haired and golden-skinned, lithe with walking and climbing; no wonder she became a legend.

Nowadays she lives in the New Forest and has there a magnificent collection of photographs of the Naga people. There is one thing odd about her collection: there are no photographs of herself. She was certainly not vain.

The army has a saying, 'Bullshit Baffles Brains'. When one commanded a company one soon realised what truth was held in those three words. The Americans had very little bullshit, so little in fact that to any British or Indian soldier they looked useless. Badly dressed with poor discipline, it was a surprise to find that they could be tough and fierce fighters. At our lowest point in November 1942, my company had been a mess. Inspected by two senior officers, we had had no guard, the rifles unprotected, lorries parked higgledy-piggledy. The only visible soldier had been a havildar clerk in loose sandals, his shirt hanging out, chasing a goat across the compound. Now my unit and indeed all the army were full of bullshit and the men had got hold of the phrase, but had not got its use quite right.

"Ah, Major Sahib," said Subadar Koshy, as we inspected the Headquarters platoon, "I have made arrangements when Colonel inspects for much bullshit — like that made by large Brahmin bull."

Cow dung smoothed over earth floors gives in the end a hard polished surface about one inch deep. As there were no cows up the Tiddim Track, pails of cow dung would be taken up from Imphal to smooth the tent floors. It left no smell. Polishing with cow dung was widespread all over India. The Manipuris used it on all their basha floors and the polished surface stood up to the rain.

That monsoon my office was in the covered verandah of one of these bashas, the floor being about two feet up from the outside ground level. There was something very cosy about working with the rain sheeting down. Day after day it fell heavy and straight as lances, at over 200 inches per year. It was rarely blown in at an angle. I can't remember any gales in that sheltered area, just the smell of the aromatic earth and of the flowered trees and the wet bamboos. The water drained quickly away into the deep ditches which crisscrossed the town and then on into Logtak Lake. There was a song just after the war:

> "Bamboo walls and bamboo ceilings,
> And the rain comes in all around."

But no rain came into our bashas.

Tea seemed to be outside all religious restrictions. Each platoon made it in the same way. They boiled the water and tea leaves in large dixies holding some three gallons. After it had boiled, several tins of Carnation tinned milk were added, together with a great deal of sugar, and then it was all boiled again for a further few minutes. One then had a delicious sweet thick brew which one drank very hot from an enamel mug. It was a drink which most soldiers remember with pleasure. After the war it was quite a problem to get back to the Darjeeling tea which my family used; it seemed so thin and tasteless.

To put the war in Burma in perspective one must realise that it was now late in 1943 and we had already spent over four years in the services. We now expected the war against Japan to last at least another six years. We were all convinced that it would take this long because we knew that no Japanese ever surrendered and they could live on virtually nothing. The war stretched ahead of us endlessly. Our youth was being stolen from us, our salad days had already gone.

In this second winter other troops had come in and close to us on the Tiddim Track was an East African company. It did not have as many British other ranks as Nigerian troops which had a staffing of one British soldier to five Africans. Evidently the War Office had found that while Nigerian troops needed a dilution of 20% of British, East Africans needed about 5% and Indian troops not more than 1% at the most and some of that 1% could be trained Indians.

There was an unexpected mutiny in the African company. This seemed a staggering event, as up to then the front had been mutiny-free. There was considerable upset and a British infantry platoon was rushed up to put the mutineers under close arrest. The army can act quickly and within two days I received orders convening a Court Martial and appointing me as President. It was a most interesting case, but because the twelve Africans accused could understand little English it was conducted in two languages. The Commanding Officer of the African company who was a weak man, was vehement in his accusations, but as the case proceeded it became clear that the mutineers had acted with great moderation. Tension had been building up and then they had disobeyed an order. The officer had repeated the order and had drawn his loaded revolver. They had rushed him and he had fired in the air. They then removed the revolver from him, put him under guard and had taken the revolver along to the nearest unit with a British Officer. They had handed it over to him and had informed him that they had refused the order of their commanding officer. It had all happened in quite an orderly manner.

As the case unfolded slowly, and my goodness how slowly a Court Martial moves in two languages, the prisoners' friend, a young officer with no legal training, began to make good his points against the official prosecuting officer, a solicitor who had been sent down from Corps Headquarters.

The legal officer was too pleased with his legal knowledge. His constant "With respect Mr President, that last remark is not evidence," began to put up the backs of the court. We really didn't care whether the remark was legally permissible or not, what we wanted was the truth. He must however, have kept us more or less on the rails as the proceedings were not thrown out by the legal department.

This was not a Summary Court Martial and so the views of all the members counted. In the end we were unanimous in our decision which was that there had been a mutiny, that there had been unreasonable behaviour by the OC and that the mutineers had behaved in a restrained manner. The sentences were very light and the Commanding Officer was sacked.

It was my first contact with Africans and I found myself liking them. My men had great contempt for all Africans. They regarded them as black savages from the jungle and they never tired of pointing out the large number of British NCOs needed to stiffen African troops.

Chapter 8

CALM BEFORE THE STORM

By the Autumn of 1943 the army had recovered its morale and discipline (it had undoubtedly lost both at the end of 1942), and General Slim, in overall command, was aching to get at the Japanese. 17 Indian Division was up the Tiddim Track to the south west of Imphal, while 20 Indian Division in the south east was forward of Palel at Tamu where they had built up large stocks of petrol and stores. The Japanese in the flat Kabaw Valley could move their troops very easily from one of these fronts to the other, a distance of some 60 miles, while for our troops, who would have to come back through Imphal, it was a movement of nearly 300 miles. It was therefore extremely difficult for us to concentrate troops in order to make a break-out. There had now been no fighting of any significance on these fronts for over a year. It must have been difficult for the Indian High Command to explain their inaction both to London and to Washington. Nearly 400,000 troops were tied up on the Burma front with as yet no tangible results.

At the end of January 1944 I heard that my brother Sinclair was severely ill in hospital in Imphal. Unable to eat for over two weeks he thinks his life may have been saved by two men. A British soldier gave him his only egg and he kept it down, and an American field ambulance driver, seeing his weak condition, drove him gently back from the front at Tamu at under six miles an hour. Nothing is too good to say about the American field ambulance drivers who went right forward into the fighting. Nothing too good can be said about them and nothing too bad about the American General Stillwell. Stillwell (Vinegar Joe) was probably the most unpleasant allied general in the war. He hated the British (Limeys) and was actually pleased when he heard that one column of the Chindits had been almost annihilated trying to carry out his orders. He did not treat his own infantry, Merrills Marauders, in the far north of Burma, much better.

I went to see my brother and found he had lost four stone in weight and was very weak. He had had bad dysentry for weeks, but was now recovering.

"Heaven," he said to me, "must be a place where everyone is constipated."

I took him for a brief drive, which when I mentioned it in a letter to my father, evoked a bitter outburst.

"You dare to waste petrol, while we strive so hard to save it. My allowance is twelve gallons a year."

When my brother was fit to move, I brought him back to stay with me close to Palel. We had a very pleasant camp site rather like the Lowlands of Scotland. Our mess tent, a little bit up the hill, looked out towards Logtak Lake.

One day when he and I were standing outside my tent three Japanese planes flew below us straight up the valley on the way to bomb Palel airfield. It was the only time I saw their aircraft at such close quarters although for two years we had spent a vast amount of effort in keeping our lorries and tents spread out to avoid aircraft attack.

Sinclair, who is over six feet tall, was down to about seven stone. Now he had turned the corner he was eating prodigiously. When I came in from morning parade to breakfast he would be on his second helping of bacon and eggs. He was putting on weight day by day and as he was so appreciative the Indian orderlies enjoyed feeding him. He remarked on the way our men moved their heads, tilting them sideways for yes. The nod is not known in India, neither oddly enough are there any words for please and thank you, the tone of the voice being used in their place. Sinclair stayed with me for over two weeks and got to know all the officers well.

"It is extraordinary," he said, "when I arrived here the whole unit looked perfectly normal but now I realise that, with the possible exception of yourself and Gordon Rolfe, all of them are in some way odd."

Late one evening while Sinclair was with us, Havildar Siwappa sent in a message asking me to come out and see Eaton Sahib. Tim was lying flat on his back in the middle of his platoon parade ground.

"What exactly do you think you're doing there Tim?" I asked.

"That bloody Havildar of mine thinks he commands this platoon. He keeps on telling me to go to bed. If I want to sleep on the parade ground I'll bloody sleep on the parade ground."

"If you wish to sleep on the ground Tim, I have no objection. Havildar, ask the Guard Commander to put a blanket over Eaton sahib if he goes to sleep." And I stumped off back to bed.

I later learned from my Indian adjutant that Havildar Siwappa had arranged that the Guard Commander on duty each night was to help Tim up the hill and into bed. Indians, if they liked an officer, could be very solicitous.

Looking back now over Tim's extraordinary behaviour, why did I put up with it? I discussed it recently with two of my officers who knew him well. One of them summed it up.

"Tim was completely loyal to the Company, was very hard working and he never did anything underhand. Everyone on the road liked him. You could not be bored while Tim was about." I am sorry to say he died a few years ago. I found the address of his widow and sent her a copy of *The Reluctant Major*. An unexpected book arrived and she found it was largely about her husband. She told me she cried and cried as she read it.

When writing this book I have at times thought I was perhaps exaggerating the foibles of my officers, but I then remember that my brother found them so extremely unusual as compared to officers of the British Army. Indian Army war-time officers came from a very cosmopolitan background and perhaps, because the Indian expects the British to be eccentric, as soon as an officer came into contact with Indian troops, his eccentricities flourished. This may not be so in the Indian infantry regiments, but it was certainly true among the services and was most marked in the Royal Engineers.

At the end of February the Imphal plain with night frosts and perfect spring days was a lovely place. The mountain sides all around were still adorned by necklaces of fire as the Nagas and Kukis burnt further ground for planting.

My brother wrote to my father: "I have just had a glorious bath in a tin tub at the mouth of my tent. The sun is sinking behind the horizon and a full moon is rising in the East. The breeze whispers across the plain bringing me an aroma of good vegetable soup from the mess kitchen."

One evening we heard the heavy drone of numbers of aeroplanes and going outside watched them towing gliders into the dusk over Burma. It was Wingate's expedition going into their forest clearings 200 miles behind enemy lines.* They looked very vulnerable.

On 10th March 1944, Sinclair went back to the 9th Field Regiment (20 Division) to join his troop. He found them well sited covering the main road at Witok and with a stream through the camp. Three nights later they were attacked by light tanks and infantry. The only two main guns which could be brought to bear were soon firing over open sights. The air was full of tracer bullets and the shouting of the Japanese. This at first caused confusion but the excellent siting of the defence barbed wire gave great confidence and a Bofors anti-aircraft gun, which could traverse more quickly than the 25-pounders, helped stop the attack. Shortly afterwards a platoon of the 4/10th Gurkhas came up to support the gunners. They had no food, no blankets and had had no sleep the night before, but being Gurkhas they dug in and settled down quickly.

By 2 a.m. the Japanese had surrounded the position completely but the shells of 8 Medium Artillery from further back were now falling on them and later they were able to bring fire down on the Japanese tanks when they stopped for the night.

"The shells are falling right in amongst them," the forward observation officer reported. "They are milling around trying to move away."

I mention the details of the Witok fight because although it was only a skirmish it was really the opening gambit in the battle for Imphal. We held the position, but five days later 20 Division moved back to Tamu where at Moreh we had built up very considerable stocks of petrol and supplies.

No one knew this was the start of a big campaign and I took the chance of the comparative calm to trek on foot from Churachandpur a hundred miles to Tiphaimukh. I took Snowden and three of my men. The President of the Manipur State Durbar, a young Indian Civil Servant, gave me letters of authority ordering the headman at each village to supply me with ten porters at the standard wage. I did not realise at the time that I was trekking through hostile country. There had been a rebellion by the Kukis after the first war and, while the Nagas were pro-British as were the Chins, the Kukis were anti-British. I got a very

---

*The clearings found by Colonel Towers.

frosty reception at some of the villages and I think I was lucky not to be murdered because at that time Japanese patrols were secretly crossing my path at right angles. They were getting ready for the attack that came in two weeks later. It was essential to their plan to cut all the links which joined our army on the Imphal plain to India.

My initials are D.R., but had been written DR, and on my arrival at each village, which had all received advance notice of my movements, I was astonished to find that the sick had walked in from miles around to see me. The first case I saw was the Kuki headman's elderly sister who had a terrible eye infection; it looked to me as though she would die shortly. Another case was an ear infection which I guessed was mastoid. I gave them both aspirin. At the next village a girl of about nineteen was brought to me with a poisoned leg. This I did know a great deal about as I had suffered badly from one three years before when antibiotics had not yet been invented. I now wanted to feel whether the glands at the groin were swollen. As my hand went up the girl's skirt I heard a slight stir from the watching head hunters. I quickly withdrew it and recommended hot fomentations and aspirin. I had no idea at the time that they all thought I was a doctor. Behind me I must have left a trail of dissatisfied and dying patients, all of whose relations were head hunters and anti-British. I did not fancy trekking back that way.

I think it was at Pansang that we nearly ran into the Japanese. I see from my report to the President of the Manipur State Durbar that the Chief suddenly turned from "a surly and aggressive attitude to effusive helpfulness". It is probable that the Japanese were close by and told the Chief to get me out of their way quickly. My request for 10 porters had at first been refused but now they turned up ready for the next stage and we went on, not suspecting that an enemy patrol had that night shared the village with us.

It was a hard trek as we were going up and down against the grain of the mountains. At each valley we dropped about 3,000 feet and climbed up again the same amount; a day's trek of twelve miles usually passed through two such valleys.

The pathways across the mountains were managed by lengthsmen, each one of whom was paid about 40 rupees a month (£40 per year). For this they kept clear perhaps one hundred miles of path, made watertight the bamboo huts for official visitors, dug away the landslides and repaired the bridges.

My three men were all Malayalis, good NCOs and very able, but faced with these mountains they were hardly able to struggle up them. They certainly couldn't carry anything. When I remonstrated with them the Havildar replied:

"Sahib, birds are made for flying, these unwashed and badly smelling coolies are made for walking up mountains but we Malayalis are made for sensible life on good flat ground."

"But Havildar, don't you find the mountains interesting and the trees and rivers beautiful?"

"Sahib, I not tell you what I think of these mountain, it too bad. Why, sahib, are we walking up and down over mountains to Silchar when there is good road and railway to that place? We could go in fine comfort."

We covered one stage a day. Snowden and I could easily have done two, which was 24 miles. The Kukis too for double pay would have done a double stage but our Malayalis, although carrying nothing, were exhausted after twelve miles. No wonder the Madras Infantry were no use in mountains.

Four days out we came on a larger village where, perched on a flattened hilltop, was a football field. The Headman asked me if I knew a particular man from London. This was the only Englishman he knew and it turned out that I knew all the family. It confirmed the Headman in the belief that all the British knew each other.

Four days further across the hills I arrived at Tiphaimukh to be met by an 80-year-old Englishman living with a pretty 16-year-old Lushai girl. He invited us to stay. He told us he had been sacked as secretary of the Silchar Club and had come up to Tiphaimukh to live far from other Englishmen. It turned out that he had known my grandfather, David Laing, who had played a great deal of polo at Silchar. We still have his silver cups. This elderly man spoke both Lushai and Kuki and he told me that a day's march behind me was a British deserter. The following day I dressed carefully, borrowed a table and chair and at a bend in the road, with two Indian NCOs at my back, sat waiting for the deserter. A young Scots boy who had not realised how news ran quickly across the hills, came down the path and found me waiting for him. He collapsed in despair. He was a Cameronian

(No. 4627191 Johnson). I did not want to take him with us on holiday so I gave him a movement order back to his regiment and sent instructions to the Headmen en route to ensure he went back to Imphal. Later I checked up but he had never arrived; I think he must have met a Japanese patrol and been killed.

While at Tiphaimukh I was asked to sort out a labour dispute. The coolies were asking for 1 anna per bag for loading the boats which were pulled upstream by elephants (see picture). The pre-war rate was ¼ anna. I called together the various chiefs and instructed the senior one to provide five men daily at ½ anna per bag and the three other chiefs to arrange the carry-down from the hills. Looking at the order, of which I kept a copy, it all seems extremely cheeky of me, but in those days British officers were very sure of themselves. In the Dunkirk campaign I had, as a second lieutenant, ordered a Belgian Major to clear the road of his horses and carts and he had at once obeyed me.

We were met at Tiphaimukh as arranged by a local boat which arrived punctually from Silchar. It came up with the elephant column which was bringing up empty boats for loading. It was extraordinary how the British administration worked so well across those wild mountains.

We spent three days on the boat, camping at night on sandbanks, and when we reached Silchar we found the Club alive with rumours of Japanese movements. The rumours were widespread and back in Calcutta at this time there was panic. There the staff of the prestigious *Illustrated Weekly of India* complained bitterly to the Chairman that, because the British had built such good railways, there was no place where they could run away and hide. The assistant Editor, an Anglo Indian, was convinced the Japanese would be after him personally. This was not an unusual reaction.

At Silchar the Club Secretary signed me in as a temporary member for the night. My grandfather, riding in from his tea estate, must have spent many an evening in those same large cool rooms. The small polo ponies (they were limited in those days to a height of 14 hands) would have been walked in by their syces and so the Club had spacious stables and staff rooms where my men bedded down and were fed.

There is always someone at a bar who relishes disaster.

"I don't suppose we will hold them," said a stooping cadaverous man of about fifty, "they are sure to push right through to Assam. I'm keeping a lorry ready for a getaway."

"We've got some good divisions up there now," I replied.

"But will they stand and fight? Look at Singapore. No real guts, that's the problem, not like in the last war." He thought a bit. "Don't suppose we will be drinking here in a month's time — wonder what the Japs will do with the whisky, don't expect they'll appreciate it." He sounded and looked more like Eeyore every minute. Evidently he was well known for his depressing views as the others took his remarks in good part.

I left him and went to see Snowden and the men. We arranged to catch the early morning train back by Gauhati and Dimapur. We had just got back up to Imphal when all hell was let loose. The Japanese had caught us short again. On 14th March 17 Indian Division was cut off up at Tiddim. Slim says, "I made a serious mistake in not ordering 17 Division to withdraw earlier."* It had not received any early warning from the outposts of V Force, of the Japanese movements. V Force in this region was recruited from the Kukis who were treacherous. They had been secretly in touch with the enemy and now not merely gave no warning of the attack but also betrayed several V Force officers and their caches of food and weapons to the Japanese. The Division had been slow in its reaction to its own scout's reports which had come in two days earlier. It stayed put for too long and did not move until 13th March. Before its troops could get far the Japanese had cut the Track in three places.

On 16th March at Tamu, the Japanese started pressing 20 Indian Division hard; then suddenly without any warning at all, on 28th March the Japanese appeared behind us at Milestone 105 on the Dimapur–Imphal road. How they got there without being seen is quite extraordinary and gives credence to Ben Bazeley's belief that an advance party had moved in some weeks before.

Another Madrassi GPT company, No. 96, was stationed at Milestone 105 under the command of Edmund Jones. They had no warning and a convoy coming up from Dimapur drove into the camp site one by one and every man was killed. The rump of the company was flown out but after the siege, reinforced and equipped with 10-ton diesels, they returned under the same commanding officer.

---

*Slim was reluctant to overrule the generals on the spot.

Chapter 9

START OF THE BATTLE

Lieutenant-General Scoones, in local command under Slim, had, rather late in the day, ordered 17 and 20 Divisions to pull back. They did not respond quickly. It was probably the obstinacy of the Brigade and Divisional Commanders which nearly made for another debacle. They had won many forward positions by hard fighting and were now reluctant to give up their gains. 20 Indian Division had only to get back about twenty miles to a good defensive position on the mountain road above Palel, but to do so they had to leave behind their oil depot and their stores which was a great loss. The Moreh depot was 2½ miles long and half a mile wide and contained vast quantities of oil, petrol and ammunition and also 200 head of cattle. The stores were worth over twenty million pounds in today's money and while some of this was moved most of it was destroyed or left behind. Sadly the cattle had their throats cut and most of the oil was burnt. The order to fire it was given on 31st March. It was a great loss and a serious blow to morale. These stores had been built up to supply two divisions and now these divisions had to be fed out of the supply depots in Imphal.

When 20 Division was ordered back, one of my platoons was despatched forward to Palel to help them and so we saw a great deal of the move. The road was still bad but as it wasn't monsoon time it was driveable. Our company was employed around the clock trying to ship out what was thought to be most valuable. We carried out some strange things for every unit had its own treasures and a large kitchen stove was one thing we carried. The distance from Moreh to Palel was only 35 miles so why we were ordered to bring out a mule company I can't imagine; it must have been a staff snafu (situation normal all fouled up). The move was a complete disaster: the mules were loaded reasonably easily but because there were no stalls, the men travelled in separate lorrries.

Gordon Rolfe in charge at the back saw them all off safely and our Jemadar at the front took them along evenly at twelve miles an hour, but with right-angle bends every forty or fifty yards the mules soon lost their footing and started to kick. Our company had wooden-bodied vehicles. The mess when we reached Palel was indescribable; hooves stuck out of the splintered sides and when we let down the tailboards, the blood and loose dung almost flowed out. One quarter of the mules were either dead or had to be shot.

The captain who commanded the company was in tears as he loaded and reloaded his revolver. His men too were terribly upset. Indians don't love animals in general like the British do, but they do develop a great affection for any horse or mule of which they are in charge. It's a very personal affection. Now in addition to the dead animals there were terrible injuries inflicted on each mule by kicks from all directions. There was hardly a mule left unhurt.

Later Gordon took the officer back to his own tent and gave him dinner and a great deal of rum. The man was as shocked as though he had lost his men and he could not talk. The RIASC was uniquely good in its training of mules. These came chiefly from the Argentine; they arrived hating all mankind but within six weeks by kindness they were changed from biting, kicking furies into brave and reliable animals, unafraid of shell fire and noise, and prepared to get into any vehicle. If led by its own driver a mule would walk across narrow swing bridges and swim rivers. The Indian driver, each of whom looked after three mules, became fond of his charges and earned their trust. Much of this training was controlled by Phillip Malins MC who still keeps his great interest in mules and is in regular touch with the present Indian Army.

The damage to the bodies of our lorries was bad and we had many planks splintered. However, our workshops sent up all its carpenters, the repairs were done quickly and the evacuation went on.

Meanwhile on the Tiddim Track 17 Indian Division was in a real mess with the road cut in three places behind them. There were six Japanese road blocks facing both ways between them and Imphal, but with a special effort the Division had been able to hang on to the Manipur River bridge. If they had not done so it might all have ended in disaster. The depot at Milestone 109, however, put up very little defence and there the Japanese captured big supplies of food, clothing, ammunition and petrol. In a few days we had lost the support supplies for three divisions.

There was now only one division back in Imphal and that was 23, which had been moved back there to recuperate from a great deal of malaria and dysentery. Their divisional sign was a crowing cockerel. Scoones, with the agreement of Slim, now took a bold decision and sent two brigades of that division up the Tiddim Track to help 17 Indian Division get back. It is doubtful if they would have got back without that help. Dare I say it, 17 Division was probably the best of all the good divisions involved in the siege. It had three Gurkha battalions: 1st/7th, 1st/4th and 2nd/5th. It also had 48 Brigade under Cameron whose troops were cut off in Burma by the premature blowing of the Sittang Bridge. The Division with the Black Cat divisional sign was battle seasoned, very tough and had a score to settle with the Japanese. I never ceased to wonder at the Gurkhas. We put up and fed a number of their riflemen when they were on their way up to their battalions. Even if there were only three of them they paraded themselves on their own. How tough and battle ready they looked beside my men.

Now only one brigade remained in the Imphal plain; everything else was committed and we all awaited the outcome of that extraordinary battle on the Track. Layers of our troops were interspersed with layers of Japanese. A year before there would have been panic but with the very much better morale now existing, both British and Indian troops held firm and battled their way back to Imphal. It took about a fortnight of extremely confused fighting and over 2,000 casualties. On their way back they recaptured much of their stores. They also brought back almost all their guns and vehicles. As they went by they all looked battle weary and Koshy quoted to me:

"Their gayness and their gilt are all besmirched with rainy markings in the painful field."

In any battle the individual remembers odd bits. Peter Longmore of 129 Field Regiment RA (now married to Wavell's daughter Felicity), told me that at Milestone 109 he 'liberated' an abandoned lorry full of tinned peaches. He informed his Colonel who said, "Peter, your main job is to get that lorry through and, by the way, try and match it with a load of Carnation milk." This he was able to do and for good measure he also collected a bulldozer which the Regiment treasured.

Brian Godfrey, who was doing a staff job with supplies, also remembers the withdrawal for an odd reason. He had an ugly bull terrier puppy, about which his orderly was always complaining. The road was cut on both sides of him and he had to climb out to rejoin 17 Division.

"Leave Venus behind. We'll be having a tough climb."

Two large tears rolled slowly down his Pathan orderly's cheeks.

"Sahib, I'll carry Wenus (Pathans can't pronounce Vs). If we leave her here they'll eat her." And so up the mountain he plodded, carrying the puppy as well as his rifle and equipment.

We ourselves were heavily involved in moving reinforcements and stores up and down the Tiddim Track. On it the lorries were moving in an almost continuous double line for thirty miles. One day finding myself in a long traffic jam, I walked forward half a mile and found that an Indian driver, not mine, had pulled out and tried to overtake the line. As a result he had jammed the whole flow of the road in both directions.

In those days I could drive backwards with ease so I ordered the driver to run back down the road and I reversed fast after him. The other waiting drivers thoroughly approved. Traffic jams are the bane of any retreat; an advancing army does not have them as the traffic thins out as its lines reach forward. In France in 1940 I had finally realised we were defeated when I came to a level crossing on which two trains, whistling and puffing, faced each other on one line, while on both roads traffic tailed back, a monumental fourways jam.

Now that 17, 23 and 20 Divisions were all back in the plain, we could take stock. In November 1942, when we had first come up, there was only one day's supply or less of food and petrol on the Imphal plain but, when we got cut off in 1944, we had ten days' supply in Imphal. This was even after the losses at Moreh and at Milestone 109 had been taken into account.

All through 1943 the Indian Army had been trying to find some way of getting back into Burma. It was a blessing in disguise that instead of us having to attack over an extended front with the Japanese able to concentrate at the danger points, they attacked and we had the advantage of defending on inner lines and could concentrate our forces where the danger threatened.

With the fighting troops drawn back, there was no use for many support troops and they were either being flown out or

Left to right. The author, Bill Greenbury (wounded in Imphal, page 88) and Bruce Rust (page 64).

Below. Letter sent on Christmas Day 1942 by photopost. It tells of the death on Christmas Eve of Jemadar Mohan Singh. Actual size as expanded and delivered in England.

Mrs M.R. Atkins
Teela
Bayham Road
Tunbridge Wells
Kent
England

Major D.R. Atkins
c/o Lloyds Bank Ltd, Hornby Road
Bombay

Date 25-12-42

My Dear Mother and Father,

Today is Christmas day and I only wish I could be at home with you. We had had quite a good party laid on with a dancing girls, a special issue of rum, extra eggs etc for the men. However one of my VCOs was killed in an accident yesterday and so everything had to be cancelled. He was a fine man, a Sikh with a soft voice very good manners and a sense of humour. Very good on lorry repair, we shall all miss him. We bury him today. I have a sergeant (workshops) with me now, a very good type of man, works hard and is intelligent. He messes with me. Eaton, Howlett myself and he had dinner here last night, we really had a very good party. I have a fire in my tent.

Love David

Pioneers on the Tiddim Track, 1943

Max Gray on the Tiddim Track, 1943. Note the type of tent we all used

A Kuki village

Elephants coming up river at Tiphaimukh with grain barges
(page 77)

The Imphal Plain, March 1944 (copyright Bennett)

The Imphal 'Keep', with airfield and behind that 4 Corps Headquarters, both dominated by the hill of Nungshigum (pages 98–101). (Copyright Bennett)

Imphal Plain looking south from Bishenpur. Logtak Lake on left. Every village of trees and huts was bitterly fought over for three months. Potsangbam in foreground and Ningtoukhong in distance (page 86). (Copyright Bennett)

Tamu road, 1944. All the peaks were fought for

George Dorrington on the Silchar Track (page 115)

Major at last. Tim Eaton, back row, with the Dutch girls.
Gordon Sheldon half hidden (page 138).

Author in point-to-point at Delhi, 1942 (page 132)

Senior staff. Back row fourth from right: Havildar Clerk Kuttappan Nair. Middle row: a jemadar, Subahdar Koshy, Rolfe, Eaton, Atkins, Dorrington.

George Dorrington, Margaret Eaton, the author, in George's 1903 Renault.

marched out along the difficult Tamenlong track which alone was still open.

We ourselves were placed a few miles down the road from Bishenpur. We took in our charge 1,800 lorries from other units which were going out. We drained down their petrol tanks and were able to retrieve 15,000 gallons of petrol for reissue.

During this period I got to know Bill Reynolds, the OC of Number 6 Indian Anti-Tank Battery which was close to us at Bishenpur where he had been told to dig in. The Brigadier commanding the Royal Artillery of 23 Division was a rather self-important and excitable man with a tendency to dramatise everything. Earlier on he had rushed up to visit Reynolds.

"17 Division is pulling back in disorder," he said, "it's a terrible mess. They will pass through Bishenpur and try and reform behind you. You, Reynolds, are the last defence in front of Imphal."

"We will do our best sir," said Reynolds.

"It's vital that you hold this position to the last man and the last round, is that clearly understood? The last man and the last round."

"I understand sir, but our vehicles are in full view," said Reynolds. "Shall I move them back?"

"You won't need any more vehicles Reynolds, this is a last ditch stand. You'd better burn the bloody things. You'll never need them again."

The whole area was quiet and Bill had not noticed any signs of panic in the troops passing up and down the Tiddim Track. He thought about his beautiful vehicles which he had looked after so well for months; it seemed a pity to destroy them. His Scots blood revolted at the idea of such waste so he sent the vehicles back and hid them among some old bashas in a bamboo compound about a mile back.

For almost two weeks nothing happened. During this time 17 Division, helped by 23, was extricating itself from the awful tangle up the Tiddim Track. Slowly the sounds of war came closer and at last one evening Reynolds' unit was lightly shelled. It caused the death of one havildar. Was the big attack coming? The next morning up drove the Brigadier again.

"Entirely new plans, Reynolds. The position is stabilised here and we are off to Ukhrul to the north east. Fifty Parachute Brigade has been broken and there is a heavy attack expected there. I want you to get away as soon as possible. You will need some new transport; inform the adjutant of your requirements."

"Actually sir, my transport is concealed down the road."

"I distinctly remember," said the Brigadier, "ordering you to burn your vehicles. Why did you disobey the order?"

The Brigadier went off in a thoroughly bad temper and this was to have some repercussions on Reynolds a few weeks later.

When the attack on the Ukruhl area had been turned back by 5 Division which had been flown in, routine began to reappear. Bill was told by his Colonel that the Brigadier was coming to inspect his battery and to make sure that his lavatories were spotless as the inspection of lavatories was the current craze. This was justified as we always had dysentry and cholera with us. Bill had first class new lavatories dug and gave instructions that nobody was to use them, the old lavatories meanwhile being concealed from view. The Brigadier arrived and was in a bad temper from the start. He seemed determined to find fault and after noticing some flies in the cookhouse went off to see the lavatories. They were immaculate and unused but as he opened the lid and peered down into the darkness below a fly flew out and settled on his nose.

"Disgraceful. Fly-ridden. Colonel, will you see that this officer keeps his lavatories in better condition in the future," said the Brigadier stumping off back to his jeep, thoroughly pleased with his morning's work. It was odd how senior officers who were not very self-confident, were sussed out by their juniors and despised.

One of the most treasured officers in the whole area was Major J.H. Williams, known as Elephant Bill. Later on I was in hospital in May 1945 and had a bed beside him. During the long afternoons he told me his story of the siege. During the battle the army really had done its best for his elephants. Early in March the Corps Commander himself had given him the order to get back to Imphal. They marched out on an unusual track and reached the Imphal plain near Palel. The strange convoy of forty-five elephants then moved slowly across the plain to the north west, resting at villages and feeding on their banana trees (all of which were paid for).

The Dimapur road was now cut as was the Silchar Track and the elephants needed a great deal of fodder which was not available, so Elephant Bill took his party out along the Tamenlong Track. He was now passing through country commanded by

Ursula Bower of V Force whose Nagas, when the Kukis deserted, had stood firm. Pioneer battalions were going out along the same track in parties of six hundred at a time. They were in complete disarray and were dangerous and starving. Williams thought they might kill his elephants for food so decided to head off along a tiny side path. He had five mountain ranges to cross, each 6,000 feet high, and on one occasion his party had to cut a path along a cliff face where he himself, who had no head for heights, had to go on all fours. Elephants can go where horses and mules are frightened to tread. In this case the elephants were led out by a magnificent 47-year-old elephant called Bandoola; without Bandoola giving the lead the others would never have faced the climb.

Ursula Bower tells me that just behind Williams a young officer called Sharpe reached a village and was told that a patrol of fifty Japanese were in the longhouse.

"Nonsense," he said. "They are nowhere near, it is just a rumour." He walked through the longhouse door and was never seen again. That party of fifty Japanese then turned back to Milestone 105 and never finally closed this last small track which however was too long and difficult to be used as a supply route into Manipur.

Williams's elephants spent four months in the Silchar area stopping with a friendly tea planter. Williams then walked them back into Imphal via the easier Silchar Track which George Dorrington and I later travelled by jeep.

Ursula Bower's V Force was invaluable during the siege as, with their local intelligence and their scouts, they covered 800 square miles of difficult mountains between the Japanese prong at Milestone 105 and the front thirty miles away on the Silchar Track. When the Japanese attack came close Ursula's men were quickly issued with Bren guns, proper rifles and even grenades; their old muzzle loaders were put away.

The immediate danger in Ursula's area came not from the Japanese but from the undisciplined Pioneer Battalions. Their journey was taking longer than expected and they had been under-issued with rations for the march to Silchar. As their food ran out they began looting the villages. Captain Albright of V Force came through and realising the problem removed one epaulette of his Captain's stars from his shoulder and handed it to Ursula. This helped her greatly. 4 Corps now realised what was happening, dropped some food to the Pioneers and also sent Ursula a platoon of Gurkhas. She was able with their help and with her own Scouts to keep the rabble moving across the hills.

Apart from the protection of the narrow Tamenlong Track which was never finally blocked by the Japanese, it was only Ursula Bower's small force that stood between the enemy at Milestone 105 and the main railway, 40 miles to the north west, which supplied Dimapur and north-east India.

Forty years later in England Ursula still receives regular visits from Nagas who regard her as their only connection with the British Raj. They still hope for help from us in their long and bitter struggle against the Indian Government.

The fighting at Bishenpur, where four VCs were won, was terrible. I watched it from a distance on several occasions — the tanks were inching up the hill track foot by foot. The two sides were often only four or five yards apart and, as the Japanese had this remarkable facility for digging in and were prepared to die where they lay concealed, it must have been as difficult fighting as any in the war.

The battle there was so complicated that it cannot easily be described. The Logtak Lake blocked off the east flank and the Japanese attack which came in from the south along the Tiddim Track reached Ninthoukhong on the plain. Here they were held in three months of bitter fighting on the lake's edge (see picture).

Here 111th Anti-Tank Regiment was attacked by five tanks of which they destroyed four. The fifth was below the guns' lowest trajectory so an officer lifted up the tail of the gun which was then able to fire at and destroy the fifth.

On the west flank there was very confused fighting up the Silchar Track which ran up 3,000 feet into the mountain. Our 25-pounders were rationed to six rounds a day so could give little help.

There was serious disagreement among senior Japanese officers, about which of course we knew nothing. The Chief of Staff of 33 Division, Murata, kept on urging Colonel Saku, whose two battalions on the Silchar Track were on the west flank, to push on faster in a left hook to Imphal. At the end of three months' fighting Saku's battalions were finished. Only 54 men remained out of his original 920. They were incredibly brave and had died where they fought. It was this sort of action that made us feel the war would go on for another six years and hence why we had no doubt that the atom bomb was justified.

Colonel Saku got some reinforcements and on 20th May the Japanese briefly got between Bishenpur and Imphal and were only ten miles from the capital. On 4th June a marauding party even came within four miles of the Palace and behind where we were located at the time. 33 Japanese Division had by then lost 12,000 men, which was 70% of their strength but yet they still continued to attack again and again.

Unlike France in 1940, and Burma in 1942, throughout this campaign there was in our army little fear of defeat. Although the Japanese were coming in from five directions, one knew that they could not concentrate their forces at any one point. It would have taken over ten days for the Japanese at Palel to get to Bishenpur, while our troops could move across in three hours. We had the interior lines of communication. In France in 1940 we had also had interior lines of communication but then we had felt like rabbits in a ripe cornfield. Day by day we were pressed into a smaller area as the Germans came closer, narrowing our space like a combine harvester cutting corn.

There was one great failure in Scoones' type of leadership. He did not keep the middle range of officers informed of what was going on. Through all those three long years of war on the Burma front, I was on my own as a Commanding Officer and was never briefed on the progress of the campaign. In an infantry or artillery unit there are a number of majors and they can consult with one another and have close liaison with the division through their Lieutenant-Colonel. The Commanding Officer of a GPT Company had the same disciplinary powers as a battalion commander but little back-up. It was rather as if I commanded a mine sweeper and yet was not kept informed of my role. Never once did the Corps Commander call a meeting of the Commanding Officers of all those varied corps units which are the vital back-up to the fighting divisions. Such a meeting would not only have kept us in touch but would have made one feel more part of the family and more eager to help the others. Montgomery's success was based on keeping all officers informed.

Chapter 10

THE SLOGGING MATCH

A new attack, which came in at Kanglatongbi, was completely unexpected, but it had no drive behind it. My friend Bill Greenbury, who commanded 302 GPT Company, had the Japanese from 15 Division break into his lines at night. Bill seized a Sten gun and led a counter attack with his drivers. They drove out the Japs, but Bill himself was badly wounded in both legs.

Out of all those thousands of peaks which one could see stretching away in every direction from the plain of Imphal, desperate fighting took place over the control of just a very few strategic ones which controlled the roads.

At Palel, with its airfield, the road went up 3,000 feet through the saddle of Shenam and in front of that there were six small peaks around which it curved. For four months the fighting raged around those peaks. Three of them, Nippon Hill, Crete, and Scraggy, were the scene of the greatest number of attacks and counter attacks. The whole of 20 Division was involved and much of the fighting took place along the narrow knife edges which ran from peak to peak. Either side could easily walk around behind any of these hills but having got there, they couldn't hold on because troops could be moved quickly against them down or up the road.

Beside the main fighting points at Palel, at Bishenpur on the Silchar Track and at Kanglatongbi, there was another battle early on at Sangshak to the north east. This was a tragic affair which at times has been cruelly misrepresented. I have discussed it with Brigadier L.F. Richards who was then a captain and held the post of Brigade Liaison Officer. He was present throughout and saw all the signals. The account which follows can not do justice to this bitter little battle but perhaps it may help to set the record straight.

I had known 50th Indian Parachute Brigade when they were stationed in Delhi. They were made up of every major race and caste in the Indian Army except for the Sikhs, who were not included as their turbans prevented them using the parachute helmet. The young officers in Delhi looked magnificent and were at all the parties. They were wearing at that time the blue parachute wings on their right pocket. I remember a memsahib at the club looking at a group of them and misquoting:

> "Young Apollos, golden haired,
> Magnificently unprepared
> For the long dirtiness of war."

It was these same officers who took such terrible casualties in the Sangshak battle where twenty-nine of them were killed and almost all of them wounded.

On 17th March the Brigade, commanded by Tim Hope Thomson, were carrying out an exercise south of Kohima. They were not expecting to meet the enemy and so had none of their heavy equipment with them. Suddenly they were ordered to concentrate on Sangshak. This was a key junction lying near the route of the enemy's attack by 31 Division towards Kohima and directly across 15 Division's thrust to Imphal. The Japanese had come in here very strongly and unexpectedly.

By 19th March the Brigade had, although under constant attack, managed to concentrate its troops around the village. Then for six days and nights continuously there raged one of the fiercest battles of the campaign. The ground was rocky, trenches were shallow, they had no barbed wire. The Japanese broke through the perimeter time after time, but each time were thrown back. The position held but only just. Sleep was impossible, water was scarce, mule carcasses and human bodies could not be buried.

On 26th March the Brigade was ordered to fight its way out. The Brigadier decided to take a route 2,000 feet down a cliff into thick jungle below. A much needed air drop at last light fortunately fell mostly into the hands of the Japanese and while they were collecting and eating this the Brigade was able to slip away. The daring plan had succeeded and the Brigade evacuated its position from under the very noses of the Japanese without further loss.

Out of the 1,850 men in the box (not 3,000 as often stated) the

Brigade lost forty officers* and VCOs, and 545 Indian, Gurkha and British soldiers killed. They carried out every wounded man who could be found in the dark. It was a magnificent joint effort by Gurkha, Hindu, Mohammedan and British, all of whom helped each other.

An odd little story comes from the Japanese side. On capturing the hill which was covered with the rotting corpses of men and mules they could not locate the body of Lt. Naka. They found that because of his bravery the British had given him an honoured burial. His sword had not been looted but had been laid beside him.

General Slim in an order of the day wrote, "Your Parachute Brigade bore the brunt of the enemy's powerful flanking attack and gave the garrison at Imphal vital time."

To put the Imphal battle in proportion with the fighting in the north, the American Forces near the Chinese border consisted of 12,000 troops of which 3,000 were infantry. These were commended by Merrill who was a good soldier. Stilwell himself seems to have done more harm than good to whatever he touched. Total casualties in the north in the whole three-year campaign appear to have been about 5,000 Chinese and 1,000 American. In the Imphal siege we lost 12,500 to the Japanese 55,000.

17 and 23 Indian Divisions had now regrouped and to my dismay my Company was sent to hold a new line against the slight possibility of a Japanese attack along a very narrow track to the north-east of Palel. This was the track the elephants had used. My Madrassis took a very poor view of being in the front line. Although they were trained in arms and we had rifles and a few anti-tank rifles of elderly vintage, they pointed out to me that it was all extremely dangerous. Fortunately nothing happened during the two days we were there. How we would have coped I have no idea, but I have never seen such deep trenches as some of the men dug. Gordon Rolfe's useless VCO had his own dug seven feet deep and we had to shovel earth back so that our men could see over the top.

My men always took a poor view of danger. On one occasion,

---

*Mike Webb and Robin de la Haye were killed leading an heroic frontal attack to recapture trenches lost to the Japanese. Richard Gillett was seriously wounded. He was carried out on a stretcher that night but, like so many others, died an hour later. They were the three whom I had known in Delhi and were all in 152 Indian Parachute Battalion.

when there was desultory shelling on the road, one of my havildars said to me:

"Sahib, I have orders to take ten lorries to Bishenpur but not possible, Sahib."

"Why, Havildar? You know the road perfectly well."

"Very dangerous, Sahib. Shells landing right on road and exploding with loud bang. Very big chance of being hurt."

"Havildar Sahib, there is an order to us to send ten lorries and so you must go."

"Very well, Sahib, I go but please not to give blame to me if I am badly killed, and Government property much hurt."

Off he went quite cheerfully and did the job which he had been ordered to do, but his was typical of the approach of these very intelligent Madrassis. On the other hand, it was one of these same Malayali drivers who, when machine-gunned with Rolfe by a Japanese plane, fired back at the plane with his rifle, while Terry emptied his revolver at it. This needed quite a lot of courage as one's instinct is to lie face downwards.

After two days we were moved in late April from our long extended line into Box Bull at Palel. This included the airfield. There were six sectors of which I commanded one under the control of a Lt.-Colonel. I had all sorts of odd companies under my command including a Bakery section and a Disinfestation unit. On my right flank was the RAF Regiment which held another sector. We had daily conferences and at our second conference the major (or equivalent rank) commanding the RAF sector made this request to the Colonel:

"Our men are not getting enough hot meals, Sir, so could you please arrange for our trenches to be taken over by the Transport Company for two hours each day in order that my men can get to the canteen?"

The rest of us could hardly believe our ears. We looked towards the Colonel. He handled it tactfully.

"I think that would cause confusion. Do you not think you could feed your men in relays?"

"Quite impossible," replied the RAF Major. "Our catering staff must have their time off and they would never stand for it."

"I'm afraid you and the RAF will just have to sort it out as best as you can," said the Colonel.

"It will be most awkward, Sir, I don't know how the men's

morale will stand up to it."

The Colonel did not reply.

The following day a very keen Indian Officer who I think commanded a Bridging unit, reported to me that, while the RAF Regiment continued to man its trenches at night, the area next to his unit manned by other RAF personnel was more or less deserted at night as many of them went home to bed. It was not, however, until the night of the 3rd/4th July, that the Japanese penetrated the defence through RAF lines and blew up eight planes including three Spitfires and two Hurricanes.

It is unfair to criticise the RAF when we owe our lives to them. They flew over 8,000 sorties into the Imphal plain and carried in, apart from ammunition, 400 tons of sugar, 1,300 tons of grain, 7,000 gallons of rum, 850,000 gallons of petrol and 43,000,000 cigarettes. A total of 22,000 tons of supplies were transported by them and also the whole of 5 Indian Division was flown in.

After the evacuation of spare troops, 155,000 men still remained in the plain. Of these, 30,000 were British and the balance Indian with a few Africans. We needed 470 tons daily.

What the army did not appreciate at the time was that the Japanese fighter plane, the Nakajima K1 43, known by the RAF as the 'Oscar', was nimbler than our fighters although ours could climb faster.

The Air Battle of Imphal by Norman Franks gives details of the RAF fight. We maintained air supremacy but at a cost. One hundred and fifteen of our planes were destroyed or damaged and of these only sixteen were Dakotas. One hundred and two RAF pilots and crews were killed. The Japanese casualties were less: 33 of their planes were shot down for certain with a further 22 probables, but the important point was that the RAF kept control of the skies.

I hardly saw an RAF plane at Dunkirk and I never saw an airfight over Imphal as they were occurring out of sight over the hills. What we all saw was the steady flow of Dakotas into the plain and also the RAF strikes on Japanese positions around the valley.

Returning to Box Bull, we were under attack there each night by small bodies of Japanese and the Colonel asked me to swing a reserve platoon across the neck of the valley so that if the airfield fell we would still have a complete defence.

Night after night the Japanese slipped through our defences and fired up at us from the paddyfields in the centre of the Box where no troops were camped. It was an extraordinary feeling watching the tracers searching for our trenches. Bullets seem to travel slowly at night; one felt one could have caught them as they arched away up into the hills. One morning two Japanese did not find their way out. Dawn came and we knew they were there but they were hidden among dry bushes. Calls to surrender were ignored and we set fire to the bushes to burn them out. They had only one grenade between so they clasped each other with the grenade held under their chins. They blew off both their own heads. It was all very gruesome and brave.

After this episode I had all the scrub on our front burned. I chose a time when the wind was blowing away from an ammunition dump near us. With the certainty of 'Sod's Law' the wind changed and strengthened, and the fire swept past my fire squad. The ammunition dump was up the hill under the control of an English unit so it was no use sending an Urdu speaker. I ran as I have never run before or since up the hill and arrived there hot, dishevelled and panicky. I found a portly British Sergeant who looked me up and down.

"Might there be some manner in which I could be of assistance, Sir?"

"For God's sake, quick, turn everybody out," I panted, "the fire is sweeping up the slope towards you. Cut a firebreak at once."

"I had already anticipated the possibility of a conflagration," he said, bowing like Jeeves from the waist. Perhaps he was a butler in real life.

"Do you mean you already have a firebreak?" I asked.

"A tour of inspection, on which perhaps I might be permitted to accompany you, will establish whether or not our precautions are adequate."

"For God's sake, have you or have you not a firebreak round the ammunition?"

"In one word, Sir, yes." I could hardly take in the sudden short reply.

"You mean there is one."

"As I assured you, Sir, the answer is in the affirmative."

As we were talking the wind turned again and the fire fizzled out. I looked around; he was right, there was an excellent firebreak. I tottered off down the hill to my tent and a long, strong glass of rum. I felt I had made a complete fool of myself.

While we were in Box Bull the Japanese were shelling us daily. We watched with some surprise how ineffectual it was at first. We must have had several thousand people in the box, and yet all their shells contrived to fall on unused areas. Later, however, they brought up several heavier guns and then it became less pleasant. Later still, when the battle had rolled back a few miles from Palel, a friend (Cecil Bendall of 64 GPT Company) went up to see if he could find the guns. They were 105s, made in England by Vickers Armstrong in 1912, and their barrels had been 'blown' by the Japs. Two of the armoured half-tracks, which had been booby trapped with small contact mines, were Mercedes Benz and the others exact copies.

About this time we got a new Colonel at Imphal. He was a red-faced and bad-tempered man who kept on badgering me for returns. He was disliked by all his Company Commanders.

"Listen, Sir," I said, holding out the telephone, "we are being shelled.

"I don't bloody care if you are being machine-gunned, get those bloody returns in."

My officers at times were very defensive for me. When this colonel came to check on us, Drurie said:

"David, don't look so anxious. Your eyes go wide like a nervous dog. Try and look confident." It was an odd remark for a lieutenant to make to his major even if I was ten years younger than him.

This colonel was the first emergency commissioned officer under whom I had served. Universally disliked, he was later to have his leg broken during a boisterous night at another transport company's mess. It was said that it was deliberate. Anyhow, we were all glad to see him go.

In peacetime, the Indian Army was an elite. It skimmed off most of the top half of those passing out of Sandhurst. This was because the pay was very much higher than in the British Army and the chances of promotion to high rank were double because of the dilution of the junior ranks by VCOs. The RIASC was chiefly recruited from officers from good regiments who had opted to change because of promotion blocks or for personal reasons. The regulars of the Corps were therefore on the whole intelligent and educated officers but perhaps with a tendency to be slightly eccentric or loners.

The hills above my position to the left were held by the Khalibahadurs, a regiment of the Royal Nepalese Army. The name means 'only the brave'. On the night of 2nd/3rd May they fired all night and in the morning it was found that they had killed two Japanese, a few of their own men, and had used many thousands of rounds. The Colonel reported this to Corps HQ and next morning Kenneth Townsend, a young British Captain from the 4th/10th Gurkha Rifles was sent over. The Colonel sent him down to me to have dinner and a bath before he went up to take command of the Khalibahadurs. We had a long pleasant evening together. That night, just before dawn on the 4th May, he was killed; one of his own sentries panicked and shot him as he was doing his rounds. It was a desperate waste.

When the Japanese attacks on Box Bull eased up we were moved back to the Bishenpur Road. Up to that time rations had been full for the infantry and two-thirds for support troops. Now they were cut to two-thirds for the divisions and we were cut to half — quite reasonable in the circumstances. We were all getting thinner day by day. At dinner I would carve a small tin of bully beef between seven officers. We had enough rice but as we had little else we were all losing weight fast and meals were eagerly awaited. Those who have dieted will know the feeling. What was absolutely maddening at this time was that Tim was quite frequently late and with food so short I did not feel I could start without him. At last he would come in.

"I say, Tim old boy," said Jimmy James, "it's not cricket, you know, keeping us all waiting, what."

"Where the hell have you been, Tim?" I said.

"A lorry broke down near Bishenpur and because of the shelling the Havildar had not fetched it in."

"All right, all right, you can tell me about it later. For God's sake let's eat now."

When Tim was late the other officers were strangely silent and it was not till after the siege that I heard the true story. Twice a week Tim was accompanying his lorries up near the fighting at Bishenpur and then climbing up to a Naga village where they were preparing him all the rice beer (much stronger than our beer) that he could carry. Because of sniping from both sides he had to wait for nightfall before making the climb.

He even continued to do this when the Japanese had by-passed Bishenpur and were for a short time astride the road between Tim and his drink supply.

Food became an obsession with everyone. A unit which was flying out delivered us two lorry loads of what looked like dried vegetables. They turned out to be chillies; they had obviously been over-ordering for many months. To carry around six months' supply of chillies was quite ridiculous and typical of the waste in parts of the army.

We may have been hungry but the Japanese were starving. When later on they began to withdraw there were dead men propped against the trees at the bottom of any steep hill — they had just sat down and died when faced with another climb. At one point in their retreat a platoon of Gurkhas established itself on the east side of the Manipur river where the Tiddim Track ran close to the river to the west. They were there for some days, firing at the Japs as they plodded back along the river bank. There was not sufficient administration left in the enemy to direct their troops to turn aside to avoid the 200-yard stretch of road which had become a death trap.

The Japanese had so completely exhausted themselves that in the final weeks we were killing fifteen Japs for every casualty of ours. Only two years before, the Japanese soldier had been dominant and had been worth at least three British or Indian soldiers. In the first Arakan battle early in 1943 we lost 5,000 to their 1,000.

From our camp near Imphal one could see and hear part of the battle on the Tiddim Track at Bishenpur and when we had been at Palel one could hear the fighting two miles away, just out of sight beyond the Shenam saddle. We were very aware that on all sides the enemy were attacking daily and that we were enclosed in an area of about thirty miles by twelve. Confidence, however, continued strong. This confidence was helped when Noel Coward and George Formby were both flown in. They gave concerts well within the fighting zones at Bishenpur and at Palel. The staff officer back in India was always fair game for those in forward areas and Noel Coward's songs on the fashionable life in Delhi were wildly applauded.

> "Sticking it out at the Cecil,
> Doing our bit for the war,
> Going through hell at Maidens Hotel,
> Where they stop serving drinks prompt at four."

and

> "He was dropped on his head at the age of two,
> So he's now on the staff up at GHQ."

Eight miles north of Imphal, the fighting at Kanglatongbi on the road to Kohima was not so intense as elsewhere and there seemed to be no chance of a breakthrough by the Japanese, neither, in spite of our defeat at Sangshak, did there seem much danger from down the Ukhrul Track. It was at Palel and Bishenpur that there was intense pressure and great danger.

My brother was forward with a Field Artillery unit near Ukhrul and, when he came back to see me, I would fill a 15-cwt lorry with material for bunkers and send it back with him. Where we were stationed we had bamboo poles 30 feet tall and 12 inches thick, out of which one could make walls, roofs, floors, water pots and even kettles. If expertly hammered, large bamboos open up into flat and pliable planks about 18 inches wide.

At Imphal the planes continued to come in to the airfield every few minutes. They were unloaded very fast, surplus troops and casualties were embarked at once, and then the planes were off. Paul Scott, the novelist, was in charge of one of the unloading sections. The target for keeping the garrison fully supplied was 300 sorties a day, but this was only achieved on two occasions. When the monsoon started it became even more difficult and on one day only four planes got through. All the time, therefore, our reserves of food, petrol and ammunition were dwindling.

One of the problems of the airlift was that the only possible lorry route to the unloading area ran right under the incoming flight path. 64 GPT Company lost a man killed when the top of his lorry was taken off by a Dakota, and after this the drivers were nervous of the road.

Petrol was vital and the officer in charge of it at Imphal (Ian Keith) found to his dismay that he was short of thousands of gallons. This may have been due to fraud back in India. His men had earlier been decanting 44-gallon barrels into cans and sending them forward to the depots at Milestone 109 on the Tiddim Track and to Moreh near Tamu. Each barrel had actually contained only 43 gallons so without knowing it he was losing one gallon a barrel. When these two big depots were both lost, petrol stocks at Imphal began to dwindle fast and it was possible to check the actual barrels on the ground. He was 38,000 gallons short. The Corps Commander, Scoones, was informed of the shortage; it was a severe blow to the garrison. Then up came the good news. Bob Elliott, who was sixty yards away from me in Box Bull, recounted his petrol stocks at Palel. In the rush of the withdrawal of 20 Division from Tamu, the Division had brought in large stocks and unloaded it in a Sub Depot where the VCO, who was only used to issuing petrol not receiving it, had not taken it into account. Bob had a surplus of 180,000 gallons. Scoones got the news that night; we had on balance 140,000 gallons of petrol more than we thought. His craggy face broke into a rare smile and he is said to have skipped. The news lifted the hearts of Corps Headquarters.

As the siege went on the petrol depot at Palel was drained dry and Bob Elliott moved to Imphal to take the place of Ian Keith who was sent off to try and supply the troops near Kohima. In the last days of May and early June every drop of petrol flown in during the day was gone by nightfall. The 140,000 gallons had been invaluable.

One of the main airfields supplying us was Agartala from where British, New Zealand and Canadian planes were flying in to Imphal. Wingate's main Chindit expedition at Broadway and White City, a hundred miles behind the Japanese lines, was being supplied by American planes from Sylhet. Kenneth Capel Cure, who I had known at Dimapur, was now in charge of the loading of supplies there. He flew in himself to the forward strips to set up the unloading sections. The fighter squadrons protecting the transport planes were at Cox's Bazaar on the coast.

It all worked well and day after day we watched the comforting sight of the Dakotas swinging in against the background of the mountains, their lights flashing for there was no need for concealment even when the Japanese 15 Division unexpectedly captured the hill at Nungshigum. This overlooked the main airfield, and Corps Headquarters nearby.

That was our real moment of danger. The Japanese from this 1,000-foot hill dominated the heart of our defence system and supply lines. It was absolutely vital to dislodge them and an attack was carefully planned. At 10.30 a.m. on 13th April the Dogras started up supported by 'B' Squadron of the Carabineers. As they slowly climbed the steep hill, the Japanese position was bombed by two squadrons of Vengeance dive bombers and then machine-gunned by Hurricanes. After that it was heavily shelled by all the guns of 5 Division. Attracted by the activity on the hill I stopped my car and watched from about one mile distant this extraordinary and tragic battle. I was too far away to see the details and the account which follows is taken from the book by Evans and Brett-James, *Imphal*.

The six tanks and the infantry, who could only communicate with each other by word of mouth, climbed slowly up the bare hillside and by eleven thirty had reached the first peak. They then had to advance in single file along a knife edge to the second peak. There are photographs of the Japanese and British staffs both watching the battle. On the British side Briggs, Evans and Scoones were there and also the Carabineers' Commander Ralph Younger who was in communication with all the tanks. The tanks could talk to him and to each other but not to the infantry just close to them. This was to have tragic results.

On the second peak the tank gunners could not depress their guns sufficiently to fire at the Japanese bunkers ten yards in front of them, so the tank commanders were forced to put their heads and shoulders out to throw grenades and fire pistols. They were easy targets for a rifle from a few yards away.

With earphones on Younger heard the reports coming in from each tank.

"Commander killed."

"Commander wounded."

"Major Sandford (the squadron commander) badly wounded."

Younger ordered Lt. Fitzoy-Herbert to take command of the squadron, but a few moments later came the report from his tank, "Commander killed."

In the space of a few minutes, five out of the six commanders fell back inside their tanks dead or mortally wounded. Then to the horror of the watchers below, the sixth tank slipped on the knife edge of the mountain, reared up and toppled over out of sight down the other side of the hill.

Sergeant Major Craddock took over command of the remaining five tanks of the two troops. Among the Dogras the senior officer Major Jones had been badly wounded and Captain Alden came up and took over. He had to climb up onto a tank to direct its fire but within a minute was also badly wounded. There were now no British officers left on the hill, and the command of the Dogras fell on Subahdar Ranbir Singh who fortunately could speak good English. He and the Sergeant Major then planned two more attacks and at last one tank was able to climb the last ten yards right up to the bunker. The Dogras with bayonet and grenade killed the last surviving Japanese. Later a Japanese sword captured there was presented by the Dogras to Sergeant Major Craddock.

This small but deadly battle was the crisis point of the whole campaign. If the Japanese had held and reinforced the hill, the airfield would have been unusable. After this setback the Japanese General Yamouchi commanding 15 Division almost gave up.

This General was a most unusual man. He would only use a Western-type lavatory and across the mountains behind him toiled his orderly carrying his thunder box. Evelyn Waugh's account of Althorpe and his thunder box would have interested him but had not yet been written. Yamouchi was a westernised Japanese who never had any faith in the attack on Imphal. He wrote Haiku, which are 17-syllable poems. One, which may be interpreted as defeatist, went:

> "The Hills of Arakan,
> I have crossed in
> my journey to the next world."

His senior commander Mutaguchi throughout early June kept giving him orders to take Imphal, which was only ten miles away.

"Take Imphal, crush the enemy, seize both airfields," were the instructions received. He hadn't a chance to do so with the troops he had under command. He lasted another two months before, on 16th June, he was replaced.

His Division had earlier on split into two sections. One of these was attacking from Milestone 105 towards Kanglatongbi at the north west of our perimeter and the other down the Ukhrul track at the north east. The height of their success was the battle of Sangshak and the temporary capture of the hill of Nungshigum. Both engagements caused them heavy casualties, and commanded by their dreamy and undynamic General, from then on they had tended to fight defensively. This division had the longest and most difficult supply line of all the Japanese columns and never had much hope of success. They were however the only troops to have some poison gas grenades for use against tanks. This was a German invention, a glass ball containing prussic acid gas in liquid form. Only one was ever used. This was when a young Japanese ran out of his foxhole and broke the glass on a British tank. The fumes were drawn in and the crew died almost instantly.

Chapter 11

THE ENEMY BREAKS

In the long months when we were besieged in Imphal we were aware that there was another hard fought battle going on at Kohima.* When afterwards I passed through the scarred hills, the old Kohima I had known had gone. The battle for the tennis court is well recorded but now I stood looking across the slopes of the mountain up which 2 Division (see Appendix III) launched so many attacks and suffered 2,000 casualties. What a beautiful stopping place it used to be and in the battle what a terrible place it must have been to attack uphill with little cover and against entrenched troops. It was on the side of the road here that 2 British Division later had carved on a rough hewn stone the words:

> "When you go home
> Tell them of us and say,
> For your tomorrow
> We gave our today."

Altogether at Kohima we lost 4,050 men and the Japanese 5,700.

The final assault on Kohima was made by the 4th/1st Gurkhas, the 15th Royal Berkshire, the 1st Queens and the 4/15 Punjab Regiment. The latter erected shortly afterwards their own memorial there and it was unveiled with full ceremony. They had a splendid record of VCs in both wars and for the ceremony in Kohima they brought up Sardar Bahardur Ishar Singh VC, OB 1 (1st Class) MVO, ADC to the King Emperor, ADC to the Viceroy, King's Orderly officer. The Indian Army was first class at giving honour where honour was due. It was this regiment whose adjutant

---

*Slim says that Major General Sato of 31 Japanese Division was most unenterprising. "I regarded him," he writes, "as one of my most helpful Generals."

(R.A.J. Fowler) before battle translated into Urdu the exhortation of Shakespeare's King John. It had a great effect on the men.

> "Come the three corners of the world in arms,
> And we shall shock them . . ."

Marian Carswell came out in the summer of 1944 and she was in time to nurse many of the casualties from 2 Division. She was issued on arrival with an old style sun topi, no shorts or slacks but with canvas shoes with canvas tops reaching right up to her thighs. They were supposed to be held up by stocking suspenders but no one ever wore them. Who in the world ordered such ridiculous things in 1944 and was it a racket with money passing? Was there perhaps some strange secret depot in India filled to the brim with materials ordered for the Boer War, and was there some weird officer there whose life was devoted to the disposal of the stocks? How else did all British troops get issued year after year with out-of-date sun helmets?

Marian was posted to the hospital at Panitola near Dibrugarh in a fever area. There they had a sick joke to the effect that, "If the patients don't have malaria when they arrive, we see to it they have it by the time they leave."

The opening of the road came none too soon. The supply of rations for the fighting troops had been reduced earlier to two-thirds and for support troops to one half but now we were getting even less. We were extremely hungry and losing weight fast. I lost about 1½ stone during the siege. Ammunition and petrol were being used up on the same day that they arrived. Prices in the village markets had first rocketed and then we had quite rightly been forbidden to buy there. There was a vast civilian population to feed of about half a million, living on rice, fish and vegetables. We ourselves had at the beginning of the siege a little herd of ten goats which the men had refused to eat and instead had made into pets. Under the pressure of hunger eight of these went into the pot, but two white ones survived the siege. I don't know why these two were so favoured but I refrained from ordering them to be killed.

The push from Kohima down towards Imphal was made against resistance all the way and the final junction of 2 and 5 Divisions only came on 22nd June at Milestone 105, that fateful place. Behind the troops came a large convoy of ammunition and food. Trust the press — they headlined it "The beer gets through."

Not nearly enough was made in England of the length of the siege. This had started on 28th March and lasted nearly three months. At the start there were over 250,000 troops cut off and if the morale of 17, 23 and 20 Divisions had not been good, it could have developed into panic. If the Japanese attack had come in with the same power fourteen months earlier it might have led to wholesale surrenders as in Singapore, and then perhaps to an uprising in India, and then . . .

Throughout the siege the press and the army information people were constantly playing down the danger of disaster. If they had played it up, then the whole world would have been watching Imphal in the same way as it watched Stalingrad. In that case we would no longer have been 'The Forgotten Army' and the breaking of the siege would have been welcomed in England with as much acclaim as the victory of Alamein.

After a poor start the control of troops by Slim and his Generals was of a high standard but the victory was due very largely to heart rending bravery shown by individuals in really terrible conditions. This bravery was the more remarkable because the young Englishman had as a child absorbed into his subconscious his parents' disillusion brought about by the slaughter on the Somme and at Passchendaele. Our fathers had in their youth seen war as a noble extension of the great vision of empire, but not so my generation. All of us had read *All Quiet on the Western Front*, we had all lost fathers or uncles, or other relatives, and all our youth had been clouded by the certainty of the coming war and the trench slaughter that awaited us.

The Japanese had not experienced the disillusion of trench war and they were therefore readier to die for their country than we were. This made the individual heroism shown again and again by British and Indian soldiers the more remarkable. To defend a position is one thing but to attack in single file along a slippery path knowing that the hidden enemy is firing at you from a foxhole a few yards away seems to be carrying courage to the utmost, and yet this type of attack was made again and again. Perhaps the Burma war was fought at a higher intensity of individual bravery than in other places where men had their companions beside them.

A great deal of heroism by King's Officers of the Indian service went unreported. Great bravery by VCOs and NCOs was duly recorded by KCOs but there was often no one to report a KCO's bravery, so it went unrecognised.

At the beginning 17 Division had been the troops most at risk and perhaps it was fortunate that the main danger of disaster fell on such tough and experienced Brigades as 48 and 63 and that General Scoones, with the encouragement of General Slim, had had the courage to send up 7 Cavalry and two brigades of 23 Division to help get 17 Division back down the Tiddim Track.

Some months later General Slim and his three Corps Commanders were all knighted by the Viceroy, now Lord Wavell. It was a laudable effort by Churchill and the King to recognise the efforts of the army but for some unknown reason it fell flat with the troops. It was too obviously an effort to please.

The first lorries to come through had brought food and ammunition, and this was followed by convoy after convoy, as many as the road would take. Like rain on parched soil, the food renewed everyone's energies and determination which had been undermined by months of hunger. Every man in the siege had lost at least one stone and this from soldiers already slim and fit was a great deal.

In the same way as the food revived the men, the ammunition flowed up to the guns. They began to fire not six rounds a day but as many as their commanders wished. Petrol also flowed again and lorries and jeeps began to move freely. The whole army was refreshed and was able to turn to the offensive.

Japanese 15 Division was already under pursuit from 2 and 5 Divisions, and was retreating east as fast as their legs would carry them. There was no longer any danger from there.

In the south, in a left hook around the Logtak lake, 48 Brigade of 17 Division moved behind the Japanese 33 Division at Bishenpur and cut the Tiddim Track at Milestone 32. From here they attacked north while 63 Brigade attacked south from Bishenpur. These attacks made little headway against an enemy which even when surrounded did not accept defeat. As late as 2nd June, Tanaka, the new Japanese commander of 33 Japanese Division, issued this exhortation to his commanders: "Now is the time to capture Imphal." His Division had already lost a further 12,000 men and his new and furious assaults on 17 Division were suicidal.

Slim wrote with particular reference to that Division, "There is no question of the supreme courage and hardihood of the Japanese soldier."

Meanwhile, up at Kohima Japanese 31 Division was under command of Sato. Even at this stage he kept on getting ridiculous orders from Mutaguchi. His troops were exhausted and starving but on 9th June he was told to join with 15 Division and take Imphal. With 15 Division already in retreat he ignored the orders and started to move back east towards the Chindwin.

While Lt.-General Mutaguchi, from his headquarters in Maymyo, was issuing aggressive orders to his starving men, he himself was living in great luxury with a Geisha establishment attached. Each staff officer had his own girl and saki flowed freely. There were different standards for staff officers and the troops they drove on so relentlessly. It was not until 11th July that Kawabe, the senior officer in Burma, ordered Mutaguchi to end the Imphal campaign and withdraw.

Now the Japanese Army was in full retreat — weapons gone, soaked with rain, uniforms tattered, desperately hungry, their hair matted, suffering from malaria, dysentery, and with maggots in their wounds. This was the end of Japanese hopes for the conquest of India — from now on they would be on the defensive.

* * * * *

Early in the siege I had been landed with an extra officer. Stevens arrived, 6 feet 3 inches of uncertainty, pomposity and familiarity. When he presented himself at my office he did not expect a welcome, but behaved rather like a large unwanted dog.

"I'm sorry to tell you Sir (snuffle), I have been posted to you (snuffle)." All his conversations were punctuated with snuffles.

In an effort to get rid of him I pulled all the strings I could with no result. It was perhaps a compliment to land an officer on us who was known to be useless. He was not bad, he was just completely lacking in common sense. He was to be with me for another eighteen months and during all that time I only once let his platoon leave the close control of my HQ and this was when during the siege I sent it a few miles away.

After a week my Indian Adjutant came to me one morning and said:

"Perhaps you might wish to visit Stevens Sahib's platoon today, Sir?"

I took the hint and we both set off at once in my station wagon. When we reached his camp site there was a milling crowd of sepoys around a lorry, most of them had sticks and there was a buzz of angry voices. Seeing me, they began to disperse and it took me a few minutes to realise what had been happening. Stevens was under the lorry and several men who had not yet seen me were still trying to poke him out with long sticks. It was a mutiny. As the crowd finally melted away Stevens clambered out, very dirty, bruised and very sorry for himself.

"Now just explain to me," I said as we sat having tea in his tent (I had sent my adjutant off to have tea elsewhere), "what's behind all this?"

"Well, I was (snuffle) beating one of the men (snuffle)," he began.

"You were beating one of the men," I said unbelievingly.

"Yes (snuffle), but only with a gym shoe."

"Only with a gym shoe." I seemed to be repeating all his words. One thing about Stevens was that he usually told the truth.

"For God's sake, Stevens, beating a sepoy is a court martial offence."

"I asked him whether he would accept my punishment (snuffle) or go up on charge to you," he said defensively. To give a sepoy this choice was quite outside his powers.

I collected my Indian Adjutant who by now had the whole story. The beating had been on a bare bottom. I got back and told Jimmy James what had happened.

"I say, bad show, what. Can't go beating sepoys. Lets the old side down," he said.

Stevens's was a Malayali platoon, similar to Gordon's and we decided to send Gordon up at once to take over. Gordon's odd sense of humour surfaced.

"You can rely on me, Sir," he said. "I'll only beat them with their trousers on."

Stevens had already been court martialled once before and got away with a reprimand. The middle of a battle is not a good time for a court martial — everyone is too busy. Subahdar Koshy, the Indian Adjutant, had confirmed that beating sepoys was Stevens's only vice; he did not go further. He once again quoted Shakespeare at me: ". . . the gods are just and of our pleasant vices make instruments to plague us."

There was so much going on all around us that I let the whole episode blow over and to the best of my knowledge Stevens never again beat a sepoy.

"He'll never be a pukka sahib," said Jimmy sadly. Pukka means true all through. "But perhaps he'll play a straight bat in future."

During the fighting, part of 66 Indian Military Hospital was moved into Imphal to deal with the typhus patients. In the campaign troops had to push through a great deal of tall vegetation. The mites of scrub typhus sit on the tips of the blades of grass waiting to seize onto any animal or man. One of the saddest deaths from typhus was that of Major Adams of the 1st Battalion of the 11th Sikhs. At night near Kanglatongbi he led his company in heavy rain through tall elephant grass to take up a position behind the Japanese 15 Division. He must have been bitten that night because shortly afterwards he contracted typhus and in spite of devoted nursing, died. Two days before he died he heard he had been awarded the Military Cross.

Typhus was a terrible disease; it seemed so unfair to catch it from grass. Martha Davies, a nurse there at the time, wrote to me to say, "Nothing in the medicine list did any good. I could only try aspirin to keep the temperature down. What was required was real bedside nursing day after day." She had had to deal with a great deal of malaria, cholera and battle wounds but typhus was the worst. After the siege some of the known areas harbouring typhus were marked:

Typhus
Keep your Arse
Off the Grass

Now the road was open Tim urged me to send a havildar on leave at once. His motive was not far to seek: any havildar returning to the company had instructions to pick up a half hogshead of duty free rum in Calcutta. Each time, when the havildar with the barrel was due back, Tim would get restless and would think of reasons to go down to Dimapur. On one occasion Gordon, who was returning from leave, was going to bring back the rum himself. Tim went off to pick him up. He met Gordon at the station at Dimapur and loaded his kit into his 15-cwt. He looked round anxiously.

"Where's the barrel, Gordon?" he asked.

"I've arranged for it to go up in a 3-tonner."

This sounded sacrilege to Tim who backed down and had it transferred across to his own 15-cwt.

On the drive up Tim kept on stopping and checking the barrel. Near Kohima it sprang a small leak but Tim was prepared and was able to plug it with chewing gum. On arrival at Imphal he took the barrel back to his own tent where he spent a happy day decanting it into gallon jars and fruit juice bottles. A half hogshead contains 26 gallons which is a lot of rum.

The narrow twisting road from Dimapur to Tamu was still mostly one track but the landslips had at last been mastered and there were more passing places. Nevertheless, it was not easy to drive, but now up this road day and night roared a stream of great 10-ton diesels each with two Madrassi drivers in the cab. On the hill sections the spare driver helped turn the wheel. We were astonished by their skill. Their accident rate was lower than that of American and British drivers. All had their bedding rolls with them and took turns to sleep as they drove. My company's casualties in 1942 had been 5% of the lorries over the edge every 130 miles, but the new drivers were better trained than ours had been. Our had also had regular bouts of malaria which so weakened them that they could hardly turn the steering wheels.

Alec Binnie, now a clergyman in Staffordshire, recently sent me information which explains why the drivers were so good. After the tragic failures of late 1942, the Motor Transport Reinforcement centres established hill driving battalions where the sepoys drove from dawn till dusk on mountain roads. It was fierce unrelenting training and all the weak drivers were weeded out. Binnie's men had V8 Fords, Chevrolets and Dodges and even some of the ten-wheel long-nosed Studebakers, which everyone so envied and which with all the wheels driving could go through deep mud.

In Imphal, the monsoon struck us in late June but the fighting troops continued their pursuit of the broken enemy. The rain fell and fell, day after day, hour after hour; there was no let-up and every little rivulet soon ran at full tilt. All of us were skilled in placing our tents so the water ran around them but the unmetalled roads again became morasses through which the troops and stores still had to be moved forward.

It was not until early in August that the Imphal battle was finished and the 14th Army moved out of the mountains and into the Burma plains. We were left behind, forgotten, maintaining that mountain road from Palel to Tamu on which we had so much experience and where we knew every weak and treacherous place. We felt we were missing out but in the long line of communications our section was the most difficult to keep in order and the Engineers responsible had asked for us to be left with them.

Tim's platoon and another small section of Engineers spent July dismantling the Tiddim Track. The bridges we had so laboriously built were pulled apart and were then rushed forward on our lorries to Kalewa and beyond. Meanwhile down the track contractors were hauling teak trees. There was only a short period between the last of the fighting and the dismantling of the road, but the Army was paying high prices for all timber and these mountains were untapped and still are. Manipuris paid large sums to the Chins and Kukis to get the trees to the roadside. Down from the Track flowed a steady stream of heavily loaded and very dilapidated lorries. New tyres were unobtainable so they stuffed old tyres with straw. Most of the lorries were discarded army vehicles and the thieving from our vehicles of spare parts, tyres and batteries became even more intense.

Tim and his men were happy up there on the track. We had built it and now we helped destroy it. Mile by mile it melted away as the engineers pulled up the culverts and loaded the great concrete pipes onto our vehicles. We were returning the tamed mountains to their former state of wildness. They are there still, untouched by anyone; it has been a forbidden area since 1947.

On the Kalewa to Tamu road, Gordon Rolfe was kept busy filling the potholes as the felted tar strips broke and tore under the heavy traffic. These strips were laid on smoothly graded cambered earth with no other foundation. It was a brilliant wartime invention. Each strip was some six feet wide and was laid overlapped like tiles from the edge of the road inwards. As long as they were all watertight and the deep ditches on either side were kept clear, the road was excellent but once rain penetrated the surface they tended to collapse quickly. Day and night, however, we had to keep the road fit to carry the traffic as the whole army's supplies flowed past us.

We were still hampered by our vehicles. We now had wooden bodied Fords but their engines like the steel bodied Fords before, also gave out at 5,000 miles. Reconditioned engines were sent up from India but these were rubbish. Nuts and bolts were sometimes left in the pistons and it was clear that some contractors back in India were making a killing. To keep our Fords roadworthy, we had to change two engines a day every day. Fortunately we had 20 of those marvellous Studebakers which went 40,000 miles or more to one engine and, with their ten driving wheels, could tow anything. How we treasured them.

Chapter 12

MOHAMMEDAN VERSUS HINDU

Conductor Snowden who had been with us since April 1943 at last got his well-deserved promotion to commissioned rank. Sergeant Goodbury was promoted to Conductor in his place, and then George Dorrington arrived, a very young workshop Captain, who had not long taken his degree at Bristol. We treated him warily at first, but he soon fitted in (see Appendix II).

He came to stay with me the other day and told me that on arrival at the company he thought he had got into a madhouse. Jimmy was the first to meet him.

"Ah," he said, "someone fresh out from the old country. How is Piccadilly Circus?"

"Still there," said George.

"Oh to be in England now that April's there."

"Well, it's December actually," replied George.

Then Tim came in, offered him a large glass of rum, and said, "You're too late, nothing here now but form-filling and bullshit. You should have been here two years ago — people dying all over the place, that was the life."

When I came in he did not find me any easier. On his first day I sent him three orders, all of them written in pencil on the green lavatory paper (known as Army Form Blank) which I always used for messages. He could not read a single one of them.

Later in the day he came to see me to have them translated.

"Come in, Dorrington," I said, "nice to have someone with us who understands Fords."

"I've never touched a Ford in my life, sir," said George.

"Oh well, I suppose they are just like other lorries."

"I've no training on lorries at all, sir."

"Good God," I looked at him in amazement, "but I was told you'd been on a six-month specialist training course."

"So I have, sir. I am an expert on 25-pounder field guns."

How did the army manage to make so many mispostings? I am sure forward with the Field Artillery there was some poor fellow, trained in repairing Fords, who was trying to repair field guns.

Evidently I looked very run down and exhausted and was bright yellow from mepacrine. By December 1944 I was desperate for repatriation, to which I had been entitled since August '44. I had had over four years abroad and as an officer attached to the Indian Army I was at the top of the list to go home shortly. I would then be due two months' leave followed by a minimum of three months in England before going to Europe. I felt finished and I was aching to leave — my letters are full of it. "Hope deferred, maketh the heart sick." It was not to be. Army bureaucracy was plotting how to keep the more experienced officers back in India.

George's posting to us was in a way a disaster for Tim. George was unusually good at pontoon (*vingt-et-un*) and we were playing regularly for high stakes — £20–£30 a night. There was no other form of amusement. A few weeks after George joined us Tim Eaton came to me.

"The bank has stopped my remittances to my wife. I seem to have lost half a year's pay at cards," he said.

Where had Tim's money gone? We each checked up and found that all of us had come out more or less square except for George.

"I thought it was a bit odd," he remarked, "when I found that in six months in India I'd not spent a penny of my pay."

George was very inexperienced at this time, and did not have quite the same control of the platoon that Snowden used to have. Perhaps because of this a major row blew up in the workshops between the Mohammedans and the Hindus. Because there were various types of artisans including tailors, blacksmiths, barbers, painters, fitters, electricians, etc., the men in the workshop were more mixed in religion and caste than in other platoons. The row suddenly flared into something ugly. The Hindus accused the Mohammedans of deliberately using their cooking pots.

I discussed the crisis with George, but as all the pots were now suspect, I could not see an immediate solution. We had however in the workshop Havildar Storeman Paranjpe, our only Brahmin. He now came up with the solution. All the cooking pots were withdrawn and handed over to him for purification. He held them for three days under his immediate care. Meanwhile the men were fed by outside platoons. Then Paranjpe re-issued the pots personally and assured the Hindus they were clear of all taint.

"Tell me, Havildar," asked George, "what exactly have you done to the pots that makes them acceptable?"

"Nothing at all, sahib," replied Paranjpe.

"You must have done something; everybody is now perfectly happy with them."

"Well, I muddled them up, sahib, so I did not myself know which were the Hindu ones and which were the Mohammedan. I made a few new dents and scratches on each one so as to confuse everybody. I then re-issued them, saying that these are the Mohammedan cooking pots and those are the Hindu ones."

We were lucky to have such a pragmatic Brahmin in our unit. Without him I think the row could have been whipped up into something quite serious.

Now, as a unit, we could get anything we wished. George and I were expert in using the proper channels, Goodbury worked the semi-illicit world of the Sergeants, both Army and RAF, Tim covered the Engineers and their stores, and Paranjpe could work the religious elements. The mark of a good unit is that it can get any job done because at a moment's notice it knows where to get the necessary materials.

George Dorrington, as a Captain REME, was entitled to hold his own orderly room. Early on he ran into the Indian's colour prejudice. His Havildar was Ghosh, an excellent young Bengali mechanic. Several times he brought up the same sepoy on charge; the man was a great nuisance, he was untidy and kept losing his tools. After the fourth occasion George asked:

"Tell me, Havildar, why is that man always in trouble?"

"What else can you expect, sahib, look at his colour. He is black. Black men are fools."

George at this time turned his attention to two derelict jeeps* and a damaged civilian car which had been dumped near us. The latter he repaired himself and we swopped it with an RAF officer for 12-bore cartridges which we used for shooting on the lake.

The jeeps were of great use to the company and of pleasure to

---

The 'winning' of extra vehicles was an established practice. At the end of the Korean War one famous unit (nameless by request) had six 'spare' Jeeps which they destroyed by driving them over a cliff into a river.

us. George and I took a few days leave and drove one across the Silchar Track. We knew we were the only vehicle using it so could take the hairpin bends flat out. The track climbed and dropped and climbed again over six ranges of hills. The suspension bridges had only half an inch to spare on either side of the Jeep. At a ferry crossing there were many hundreds of butterflies settling on damp sand. The Nagas told us that a Japanese officer was buried there; the decomposing juices were attractive to the butterflies. What butterflies they were, some deep black, some of brilliant blue and gold, some with transparent wings and many over six inches across; an entomologist's dream.

In Silchar we stayed with three different Scottish tea planters, all proud of their efficient tea gardens. One of these gardens was my grandfather's old plantation which he had once defended against an attack by the Lushais. During the attack my grandmother had sat with a loaded pistol ready, if necessary, to shoot my mother, uncle, and herself. I walked around the small hill on which the spacious bungalow was built. My grandfather had moved around the garden from danger point to danger point with his rifle, supporting his staff who were armed with his twelve bore shotguns. I felt very close to him.

In 1944, the headgear of officers was altered from the peaked cap to the Australian bush hut turned up on one side. This was a most excellent hat for the area. It was rainproof and strong, and far better than the floppy green one which came out in 1945, and was known as the 'cabbage leaf'.

Having lost one set of uniform in France, a second lot when my tent was burned down on the Tiddim Track, and my other clothes when an ammunition ship blew up in Bombay, I now wore exactly the same clothes as the sepoys. These were of good quality and very cheap. Everything was a dirty green — vests, pants, towels, etc., so that when hanging on bushes to dry, they did not show up from the air. The standard cellular bush shirt was well designed, and as we had a durzi (tailor) on the strength, all my officers and senior NCOs were very well turned out. In the Desert from about 1942 officers had taken to wearing coloured scarves but in the 14th Army we were only permitted to wear khaki scarves of silk or cotton. These looked good, felt very comfortable and also protected the back of one's neck from mosquito bites.

The countryside continued to be an unfailing source of pleasure.

The hills around India and China have far more flowers and shrubs than anywhere else in the world. When the last Ice Age started, the flora from Europe and Russia marched south to avoid the encroaching cold. Plants, says the great naturalist Kingdon Ward, are territorial aggressors and empire builders; they fight each other for the possession of ground. Much of the invading northern flora died in the Sahara, or in the cold of the Himalayas, but some of it slipped through valleys on either side of the mountains and crept into India and Africa. Once through, it quickly established itself all across the north of the sub-continent. Ten thousand years ago when the Ice Age relaxed its hold, the southern flora which had been pushed down to the bottom of India started driving the northern flora back from whence it had come. In the ensuing battle many northern plants took refuge in the foothills of the Himalayas and up the slopes of the mountains of Burma and China. As a result, almost every tree and shrub seen in England can be found in India and China. Roses, lilies, buttercups, daisies, raspberries — they all grow there, as do the southern plants and that is why the area has been such a treasure house for botanists.

I now found some crab-apple trees and to the surprise of my company turned cook and made 60 lbs of crab-apple jelly. It was very much valued in the area and a pound pot was a welcome gift.

About this time I was transferred to the Indian Army proper. This had some disadvantages which caused me to write a letter which came to the notice of Mountbatten. The details will be found in Appendix I. Nothing particular seemed to happen about my letter, but, when on leave in Calcutta I called in at the SEAC offices, I was ushered straight up to Frank Owen, the Brigadier editor.

"So you are the man who nearly lost me my job," he said. "Your letter really upset them in Delhi; they sent a Colonel down post haste to see me. I was told I had committed a gross breach of conduct and had interfered with Army policy. It's all right now but to get off the hook I had to refer the matter up to Mountbatten himself. I told him I believed your letter dealt with a genuine army grievance which you had accurately set out."

I listened amazed. What astonished me was that whenever I was involved in any serious row, such as when at GHQ I ordered too much rum, there were no preliminary rumblings before the storm broke. My personal file must by now have been pretty thick.

The rum order, the shakapara biscuit farce, the sending of all India's flour to the wrong port, the notorious breakdown of my Company in 1942 and now this letter — I certainly wouldn't try for a regular commission. I sent copies of my letter to my father and my aunt, both of whom forwarded it to their MPs, and both of these put down questions in the House. Leo Amery, Secretary of State for India, answered the separate questions personally before the House on different days. As a result the conditions for most officers were changed but the terms expressly excluded forty or so officers, of which I was one. Frank Owen and I discussed it and thought this exclusion was deliberate by some officer in GHQ who we had got into trouble. There was, however, no point in doing anything further but the episode has left me with the belief that if you have a good case you can get it taken up in Parliament.

Mosquito drill was still vital and each evening one automatically oiled the backs of one's ears, forehead and wrists with anti-mosquito cream. Each man carried his own tin of cream. The order still existed that men before going to the lavatory should cover their bottoms in cream, but this was impossible to enforce. Guards at night continued to wear long cotton gloves and a khaki net mask like a bee hat which fell over the tin helmet and tucked into the neck.

Christmas 1944, with the feeling of victory in the air, was a day of exhausting but pleasurable feasting and drinking. Indians tend to overeat on feast days even more than the English. We had the VCOs to lunch and gave them duck pillau (the ducks shot by George and me on the lake). Then the NCOs down to Naik came to tea, which included hot rum punch, made of rum, lime and pineapple juice. We also introduced them to snap-dragon with burning brandy, and had a small Christmas cake with candles. In the evening we had the BORs into dinner and a goose. Conductor Goodbury, already rather drunk on his arrival, fell asleep at the table. That Christmas Day every British soldier in the 14th Army had chicken or goose for dinner.

The next day Area Headquarters asked all the senior officers in for a party and as I now knew most of them it was enjoyable. When I arrived the Brigadier spoke to me about a letter I had written. I had, while the local Administrative Commandant at Palel was on leave, acted in that post. Into my tray had dropped a letter from the Brigadier: "Did the Commandant consider Major Atkins' name should be put forward for an MBE." I replied: "I consider the award to Major Atkins of an MBE would be most suitable. He is a hard working and efficient officer. Signed D.R. Atkins, Major. Acting Administrative Commandant, Palel."

The Brigadier was not all that amused.

"You don't take things seriously, Atkins."

I did not get the award.

Early in 1945 I found mushrooms out on the aerodrome at Palel. I picked these and brought them back to the officers' mess for cooking. The orderlies were horrified and refused to serve them; they assured me they were deadly poisonous. I showed the mushrooms to the others and, encouraged by them, I ate one mushroom and came to no harm. From then on we used them regularly. This was much talked about by the Company.

Shortly afterwards the Havildar clerks gave a dinner party for the King's Officers. As I was about to start my main course I saw on my plate a large flabby piece of toadstool. I probed around and realised that most of the vegetables were various sorts of toadstools. I asked Havildar Kuttapan Nair what they were.

"We have arranged special treat for British Officers," he replied, "and have searched all hills nearby for mushrooms. We have got for you many different colours and shapes, all in lovely curry."

"Are you eating them yourself, Havildar sahib?" I asked.

"Oh no, sahib. We Malayalis do not eat mushrooms so see, on side table, different curries for British and Indians tonight."

I put down my fork and spoon.

"Your efforts are much appreciated Havildar Sahib, but if you will be so kind, please instruct the orderlies to withdraw all the plates with mushrooms on them, and may we now share your curry."

I think we had a lucky escape.

Chapter 13

END OF THE WAR IN EUROPE

We heard of the end of the war in Europe at 11.00 a.m. on Tuesday 8th May 1945. That afternoon we bought up all the local chickens and vegetables we could get hold of. Our own Victory party was the same evening but next day we gave all 450 of our men a magnificent feast of chicken curry, vegetables, dhal, poppadums and the sweet treacly pastries that Indians love.

Our own food had improved since we had elected George Dorrington as Mess Secretary. He was a good cook himself and he had settled down to teach our mess staff how to make fruit flans and fruit pies. We gave party after party and George, who kept a diary, tells me that on 17th May we gave Jimmy James his farewell party which developed into the water fight where I cut my hand. Then on 7th June came Tim Eaton's party on his promotion to Captain. He was very popular on the road and officers came from far and wide to the big RAF mess we had just taken over. His sense of humour was as odd as ever. I called on him for a speech and in reply he kicked the RAF bar several times with one foot, while rocking on the other.

"What does that remind you of?" he asked. None of us knew.

"It's a man with a wooden leg, having a girl up against a fence." That was the whole speech.

Tim Eaton's promotion was also popular in the company and the officers' party was shortly followed by a party given to him by all the VCOs and NCOs. The company *esprit de corps* was now magnificent and all our men were proud of themselves. Only two years before we had been the worst GPT Company in India.

At these parties one of our guests was always Taplin. He commanded several hundred labourers. On one occasion one of our lorries went over the edge with thirty of Taplin's men and then he showed a different side of himself. He was fit and strong and carried up many of them himself. They died very easily that day, even some of the uninjured died, presumably from shock.

"Bengalis," said Taplin, "have the least will to live of all Indians. No Punjabi, Gurkha of Malayali would die so casually."

The Bangladeshis are a race apart from the rest of India. They rely for survival on the highest birth rate on the Sub-Continent, and were not recruited into the army during the war.

By now I was very senior in the area and was appointed to take a number of Courts Martial. One was of considerable interest to the Hindus. A Naik had called a Jemadar a 'Manki Chod'. Our job was to find out, taking into account the background and religion of both the Naik and VCO, how serious the insult was. For example, it would be difficult to establish the necessity of a Court Martial if a British soldier called a senior NCO by certain well known four-letter words although it would of course be a chargeable offence. We took evidence on what exactly was meant by the expression and how it was regarded. It turned out it was the worst insult possible to the VCO's mother. We found the Naik guilty and reduced him to Sepoy. Subahdar Koshy who as Adjutant was privy to everything that went on, found the right quotation.

"That, in the Captain's mouth, is but a choleric word which in the soldier's is flat blasphemy."

"Most interesting, sahib," he went on, "that same rules apply in this army as in Shakespeare's time."

I have used 'manki chod' once or twice since but never in the army. On one occasion when I saw some Indians throwing rubbish out of the window of a stationary taxi in Shaftesbury Avenue, I opened the door and called the three of them 'manki chod'. They were struck completely dumb and shrank back into the cab. It is a dangerous phrase to use, but my goodness, it is effective.

I had now done over four years in India and felt I had had enough. My health, which had at first been really sparkling, was deteriorating and I began to get carbuncles.* These are most painful and unsightly things to have. It was particularly unfortunate that an order had come through from SEAC headquarters that

---

*Slim had an investigation done on the poor health of the 14th Army. It was found that after a year in the area food passed through men without the normal nourishment being extracted from it.

no shirts were to be worn in the day time. One wore one's badges of rank on the left wrist on a cloth band. On top of everything, as my resistance weakened I started catching every skin disease under the sun, not merely dhobis itch which was endemic in the army and easily cured, but obscurer fungi. I always seemed to be covered with patches of gentian violet, the universal skin disease cure, and I found inspecting the troops and guards embarrassing as the Indian is morbidly interested in disease.

I did not like going out white and half naked to take a parade of brown skinned men all of whom seemed to fit into the countryside better than Europeans. Some of an officer's dignity, particularly if he was fat, seemed to vanish along with the top half of the uniform. We were now dressed in heavy sepoy boots, cloth gaiters, long dark green trousers kept up by a webbing belt holding a loaded pistol, then nothing until an Australian bush hat pinned up on one side. One of the good things about being stripped to the waist throughout the day was that prickly heat virtually disappeared.

Talking of odd diseases, two of my men got guinea worm. In this disease the worm puts its head out of the man's bloated leg. It has then to be caught and rolled onto a twig which is taped down. As the worm struggles it loosens itself, the twig is turned and slowly over several days the long worm is drawn out; I think they can measure up to two feet.

It wasn't until 1987 that I learned, while reading *The Longest War*, that there was an area near Palel known as Typhus Hill. Why were we not warned at the time? It was on this same hill that we ended up after the siege. Fortunately I was very aware of typhus and was enforcing strongly the order to treat every man's uniform. Every week all ranks attended typhus parades. Each man had a mess tin of anti-typhus oil at his feet and all his clothes in a pile beside him.

"Company, hold up trousers."
"Left trouser leg, dip, stroke, dip stroke."
"Right trouser leg, dip, stroke, dip stroke."
"Seat of trousers, dip, stroke, dip stroke."

Two fingers were dipped in the oil and wiped dry on the clothes. By the end of the parade all our clothes were oily and smelly. Fortunately as we all smelt as bad it didn't worry us much.

Looking back on it, I think the treatment saved many lives as on that hill we must have had typhus mites all around us. They were lying in wait on the tips of the long grass ready to leap onto us. Even with our precautions we had some forty casualties, including twelve deaths.

The mepacrine tablets we were all taking turned us bright yellow. The rumour was that they also made one impotent, and as a result many men tried to avoid taking them. We had therefore to give them as a parade. Each man put one in his mouth, took a drink, and then had to say his name and number; this stopped the man pouching the pill in his cheek. The total result was that when one went back to India one was not merely bright yellow but also smelt like a rat — not conducive to romance.

I was due for another leave and an engineering officer, call him Donald Smith, offered to give me an introduction to a lovely young girl who had her own houseboat in Srinagar. She took in guests but was not 'available'; still, there was always hope of a lucky break, perhaps she liked yellow rats. I wrote and arranged a visit, getting a very nice letter in reply. I was looking forward to it vastly and was greatly envied. A letter then arrived. It started:

> "Please oh please David tell me where Donald is. He promised faithfully to write regularly and said we'd get married. I am three months overdue. What am I to do. Please what am I to do. Please help me. I am so looking forward to your visit and then I know you will help me decide what to do for the best. Oh David I do so long to meet you."

Shades of Lady Hamilton's letter to Greville when at the age of sixteen she was deserted and pregnant. I cancelled at once, but felt I should have gone; a delicate and lovely girl in distress was waiting for a young knight on a white charger to ride up and rescue her and I had turned that charger aside.

Now that my visit to Kashmir had fallen through, I still had my leave due to me and I wrote to the Viceroy's social secretary in Simla to ask if I could go and stay there again. I received back an invitation to the Observatory annexe which the Viceroy had put aside for five officers at a time to take their leave. It was the former house of the Viceroy's personal assistant, and was now run by Mrs Stevens. It was a delightful place with fine china, polished tables and first class staff all clad in the Viceroy's personal livery. The only discordant note was my face which was such an unpleasant yellow. Girls still found me amusing but at a distance. I still knew three Simla girls and as they introduced us to others, the five of us had some most amusing dinner parties with Mrs Stevens presiding. She was allowed at her discretion to use the Viceroy's wine stocks and, as we were all back from the front, she supplied the sherry, wine and liqueur for us all as the Viceroy's guests. By day we all went out on bicycles for picnics along that lovely fir clad ridge to Mashobra, mentioned by Kipling.

At the end of my leave I stopped off in Delhi and had a very enthusiastic reception from my old office, most of whom were still there. My old bearer Chutan was horrified at my appearance. I had no service dress or service cap but was dressed just like a sepoy. He gave me a thorough telling off.

"If your Daddy could see you now, Daddy would say, 'That is no son of mine, that man dressed like beggar. He is not like pukka Major sahib'."

Jack Jones, my first captain, was now a full colonel and was rigged out with the red tabs and the red-ringed service cap of the senior staff officer. He had a strange story to tell me. The Quartermaster General had sent for him and showed him a letter he had had from Jemadar Rudolf's protector. I use the term, but not in any sexual sense. I never met this retired officer, but he had taken the Jemadar under his wing when Rudolf was a young boy and clearly had the highest opinion of him. He had now written to the Quartermaster General saying that he had it on the best authority (Jemadar Rudolf's) that Major Atkins was selling Government property in Manipur state. The letter ended, "We all know that there are Englishmen like Major Atkins in this expanded army and they must be rooted out."

The Quartermaster General asked Jack what I was like and what Rudolf was like. It was most fortunate for me that Jack was there, and that the enquiry was stopped at that point because unknowingly I was going back into bad trouble.

On the way from Delhi, I stopped off at Lucknow to discuss our company records which seemed to be in astonishingly good order. While there I was informed that I had the right to award some ten 'jungi inams' (war awards), each of which gave a pension for life of £15 a year. When a year's normal pay is £30, this award was considerable. This was a great pleasure to me and I allocated them to our best soldiers.

I then went on down to Calcutta and stayed with Sir Cyril Gurner, who, with my father, had re-planned Calcutta in the 1930s. Together they had wiped malaria out of the city by filling in all the open ponds with earth taken from a new digging; this they turned into 'The Lakes'. It is landscaped and is still I believe one of the prettiest places in the city.

On my arrival back from leave I was staggered to find that I had been accused by one of my VCOs of misusing Government property. This South Indian VCO, a hard working and reliable man from a very poor family, had made his way up by scholarship. Families are extremely important to Indians and if they gain a position of authority, it is considered honourable to assist relations by appointments and by gifts. Nepotism therefore is rife. This VCO had been found sending parcels of food back to his family. It had been reported to me and I had warned him that if he did it again I would court martial him. He did it again, was caught, and I put him up for Court Martial. In view of his excellent service to the company and the army, I think this was a mistake. I should have posted him away on an adverse report. As it was British officers' tinned food he had stolen, the offence did not carry the same impact as if it had been Indian food or clothes. Court martials for VCOs had to go to Area Headquarters and on paper the case looked weak unless one knew it was a second offence, which fact could not be shown.

While I was away on leave this VCO had listed everything I had done which was outside strict army regulations and sent the information direct to the Brigadier. He accused me, amongst other things, of giving free clothes to my brother, who had come back from the front with torn trousers, and of giving a pair of boots to Colonel Tarver without charging him. Tarver had died a few days after the issue to him of the boots and in order not to confuse his estate, I had cancelled the small bookkeeping entry. Another offence was the destruction of a leather jerkin to make mosquito boots for an officer. We all at night wore long boots made of rubber and cloth, but Tim had developed a bad skin infection on his feet and the doctor had sent me a note saying he needed light leather boots. I had therefore given orders to have these made up from a driver's jerkin. Fortunately my head clerk had filed the doctor's note.

When I got a letter from the Brigadier convening a Court of Inquiry into my actions, I stormed down to see him, got an immediate interview, and asked him to cancel it.

"I am not going to do that, Atkins," he said. "If I did, I would never be able to look at you again without wondering whether or not you were a wrong 'un. I must clear my own mind, and that's for your own good too."

The news of the Court of Inquiry had, of course, got out to all my men and was the cause of great discussion and gossip. Nothing in the Indian Army could ever be kept secret. The Court assembled; it consisted of three King's Officers, and I duly appeared before it. It was held in my own lines so they could call easily for witnesses. I had been accused of misuse of ten items of Government property and, in every case, the facts were correct. I have the findings of the Court, which were:

"The court finds that the Subahdar is vindictively bringing trivial counter charges against his Commanding Officer as a result of himself being accused of misconduct.

During the period of over three years in which Major Atkins has been on Field Service several minor irregularities have occurred but these were occasioned by the conditions of service prevailing in this theatre of war.

The court is of the opinion that the Company is run in an efficient manner.

Signed Major L.W. Davies R.E.
       Capt. Forret R.E.M.E.
       Lt. Whitby R.E.
       I concur H.R. Officer   Brigadier."

The result was a tremendous relief to me as I knew I had broken the strict letter of regulations hundreds of times but always for the good of my company. However, a nit-picking Brigadier might properly have court martialled me.

Chapter 14

FORGOTTEN AND LEFT BEHIND

The war had entered an entirely new phase. We were now so dominant in Burma and moving forward so fast that Imphal was becoming a back area. There were now quite a number of nurses about the place and when I detached Gordon Rolfe down to Area Headquarters, to the envy of us all, he collected one. With several hundred officers to every girl it was very clever of him, particularly as many nurses seemed to like high rank in their boyfriends. Madeleine added to our mess in many ways; she restarted the flowers we had let lapse and also produced some china teacups.

The CO of a nearby remount company about this time gave an excellent party. It was a full moon and we all had drinks by the lake and then those of us who could ride cantered across the paddy fields, jumping the banks and ditches until we reached a small steep hill, up which the horses clambered.

Indian sepoys love a party and the remount company had put on a remarkable show ('tamasha'). At the top of the hill there was a large bonfire with chairs, tables, and rugs arranged around it. The horses were tethered facing inwards watching the fire and the men were seated opposite us. Dancing girls arrived and drink flowed freely for all ranks. As the girls danced, rupees were placed on men's heads and the girls would take the rupees, giving the blessing by circling their hand over the man's head. Many rupees were tucked into the horses' browbands and the girls, in order to give the blessing above the head, had to stand on chairs. One young girl with a gentle face and wide eyes, was terrified of the horses and, when one of them nudged her, fell off the chair. She ran to her mother for protection but was sternly sent back to collect the money and give the blessing.

Our Headquarters were at Palel and from there we kept the road in good order from Imphal to Tamu and forward to Kalewa.

There was not a difficult or dangerous spot on the road which my men did not know. We now had some Dodge tipping trucks, and our drivers' control of them at problem spots was excellent, particularly bearing in mind that day and night we could never block the flow of traffic. The NCOs were now so experienced and the Engineers so good, that the job ran itself, and George Dorrington and I spent many an evening shooting and sailing. Our sailing boat was made from two derelict Ford bonnet covers.* These were already shaped like a canoe and formed the bow and stern. A 40-gallon barrel cut in half made the middle of the boat and this had a liftable centreboard. With parts of a torn tent for the mainsail and jib, she went well to windward, and I taught many of the officers and VCOs to sail.

The boat was good girl-bait. At one party with a hundred men and only one girl, I stood on a chair to locate her. I beavered a way through the crowd and reached her. Someone was saying:

"I say, do come to our mess thrash, we've got some real Scotch."

I butted in, "Why not come sailing in a dinghy?"

She turned to me in surprise.

"In a real boat, sailing, really sailing? I'd love to, I adore sailing."

She was a bit surprised to find the boat was made of tin and the seats were two old food boxes but she sailed it with skill and enjoyment.

Shooting in the winter on the shallow Logtak Lake was some of the best in the world. We shot from canoes and would bring back enough teal and duck for all the headquarters and workshop staff. The first time I brought back twenty or so water-fowl, my men looked at their bright and varied colours with astonishment. I must have had there four or five different types of teal and duck.

"These must be tame birds, sahib," said a havildar. "Did you buy them in the bazaar?"

Subahdar Koshy was astonished but quickly covered it.

"Do you know, sahib, what is the opinion of Pythagoras concerning wildfowl?"

"No, sahib, I don't and I can't believe he had one."

---

*Did we misuse Government property? I asked George this recently. "No," he replied. "Remember how we were urged by HQ to make amusements for ourselves and our men."

"Yes indeed, sahib, strong opinion which links in with good Hindu teaching. Shakespeare says, 'Pythagoras thinks the soul of your grandmother might inhabit a bird'."

It took me some time to trace it, but it comes in *Twelfth Night* as a rather odd joke.

The Manipuris of one village kept a large number of clay pots floating loose on the lake. Girls using special pots with eyeholes in them would move carefully across the shallow lake bed towards the ducks as they fed amongst the pots. Reaching a duck they would pull it quickly under water and drown it silently. Each girl could collect three or four in an expedition.

Winter was the time for ducks and geese as in the summer they flew over the Himalayas to Siberia, there to nest and feed.

Although we were working our lorries hard the men had one rest day a week. We had been up on the frontier so long that it was very necessary to think up activities to keep them interested on their day off, so we had all sorts of competitions. On one occasion my officers and I, armed with a light sandbag, took it in turns to defend against all attackers a pole over a pool of water. This was very popular and although all six of us ended up in the water, we must have put forty or fifty of the men into the pool before the last of us emerged soaking and bedraggled. The things we did for England!

The canteen facilities for the British and the Indian soldiers were excellent. A packet of 10 Players cigarettes was 2½ annas (about 2d) and the Women's Auxiliary Services Burma (WASBies) visited all of us. Their stocks included the great favourites, jam and tinned fish. In addition one of our Naiks ran our own canteen. I am sure he was honest and as our turnover was well over £2,000 a year, it gave our regimental fund £200 to play with, a lot in those days.

A great number of dogs had been left behind by the advancing troops. Most of these were in bad condition and because of constant rabies scares it fell to our lot to have to shoot some. One however was a cross between a labrador and a red setter.

"I'm having no more dogs," I said. "I had to shoot my last one. We'll have to shoot this one too, unless . . ." George took it, and gave it the odd name of Busti. Soon, under food, care and affection, Busti shone like gold and regarded George as his special property. We took him to Singapore with us where Busti with his waving tail graced the stately Clubhouse which we occupied.

Now that the battle had moved away we had few alarms and excursions at night but one midnight up roared a motor cyclist. I was to report to the Colonel at once.

"Sorry to wake you, Atkins, but the brewery at Mandalay has been captured intact. We have to send an officer down by plane at 6 o'clock this morning to take 20 bags of yeast to Mandalay Brewery. Send someone sensible. He'll be flown straight back by the same plane, so he'll be back for lunch."

How could I have been such a fool as to believe him. I went back, got Gordon Rolfe out of bed, and explained the job to him.

"No need to take anything with you, you'll be back here by lunch time."

How could he have been such a fool as to believe me.

Gordon got to the airfield, found the bags of yeast and two American pilots.

"Hop in, bud," they said.

Gordon hopped in and sat on the bags of yeast. The flight to Mandalay was only a little over one hour and Gordon was then decanted with his yeast on an entirely empty airfield. Not a man or lorry in sight. Three hours passed and another plane came in. It was met by four lorries and unloaded.

"Can you take me to Mandalay?" Gordon asked the British Sergeant in charge.

"Not a chance, sir, and I wouldn't stay here if I was you. The Japs are only two miles away and at night they patrol this area. Why don't you hop into that plane; we'll help you load."

That plane was going to the Arakan, completely in the wrong direction. By 8 o'clock in the evening Gordon was in the Arakan, three hundred miles to the south. He had had no food all day and had none of his equipment with him. He was sitting on the twenty sacks when up drove a jeep. He recognised the driver, an old school friend.

"By God, it's Gordon Rolfe. What the hell are you doing here?"

"Trying to deliver these sacks of yeast to Mandalay."

"You've come to the wrong airfield. Mandalay's in Burma. This is India."

"The thought had struck me."

"Where's your kit?"

"In Imphal."

"But that's miles away."

"That thought had also occurred to me."

Two days later a very tired and bedraggled Gordon arrived back at our mess; he had flown in five planes.

"Back by lunch time," I heard him telling George Dorrington. "The Major told me I'd be back by lunch time."

Never be parted from your kit was a golden rule and another one was don't believe all that senior officers tell you.

Instructions had come from SEAC that we should begin training the men for peace. We started debates, one of which was on the subject of whether or not the British should get out of India. Conductor Goodbury was the main advocate that the British should stay for many years. Only someone who was not an officer could have spoken so frankly.

"You'd make a proper bugger's muddle of it; too much quarrelling and too much bribery — yes, it would be a bugger's muddle. You are not fit to run a fish and chip shop." This was his standard expression. None of his audience had ever heard of fish and chips.

His speech was heard in silence and by me with some anxiety. At the end it was clapped good-naturedly. Indians are very tolerant and they liked Goodbury. The voting however was about five to one in favour of our getting out. One of the odd proposals that night which had great support was that units in the Indian Army should have all Indian officers, except for the Colonels and Quartermasters, who should continue to be British. This showed their trust in us was still there.

My own personal contribution to peacetime training was a lecture on two subjects which I gave to each of the six platoons. First I advocated the killing of sacred bulls. As no bull in India is ever killed by a Hindu, these useless animals are equal in number to the cows. They wander about everywhere unhindered, eating fruit from the stalls, and vegetables and grain crops from the fields. They produce only one thing — dung — which is patted into little cakes by women and used for fuel. Dung cakes marked with girls' fingermarks can be seen drying on the walls of every hut. This part of the lecture produced considerable upset and dispute among the men; it struck at one of their main religious beliefs. It was sacrilege and I would not have got away with it if they had not known me so well and regarded me as a bit of a joke.

The other subject on which I spoke was birth control. The men now understood about condoms, but only regarded them as preventers of disease. Now in my lectures I suggested that they cut down their families to two or three children only.

"But sahib, many children die young. Much illness. The gods bring us cholera and disease. Death comes and suddenly all children gone. Who to honour us and bring foods in old age if all children dead?"

Years later I noted two of Mrs Ghandi's main teachings were the killing of sacred bulls and the use of birth control. Too many bulls and too many children even now drain India of its food and prosperity.

I see from my letters to my father that the strategy of the Chiefs of Staff at that time was based on the expectation that the Japanese war would continue to 1953. Both America and England were planning the gradual demobilisation of long-serving soldiers and their replacement with younger men. We all, therefore, long before the Bomb, got our demobilisation numbers which laid down the order of release of each man. It was a first class points system, which was based on a mixture of months of service and age. It was personally approved by Winston Churchill. I cannot remember how the points worked, but they were very fair. We all studied these tables with great interest. My own demobilisation number was 23.

Those who now object to the use of the atom bombs on Japan never take into account that if they had not been used there might have been a further seven years of fighting. This would have completely exhausted the world and caused death by starvation to tens of millions.

Chapter 15

THE ATOM BOMB AND PEACE

The news of the Atom Bomb came absolutely out of the blue. All other events in the war had thrown long shadows in front of them. By 1938 I had been convinced that war was inevitable; later we had guessed about the Russian invasion and had half expected a Japanese attack, but now — suddenly the war was at an end. We would all be free soon, but free to do what? Many officers bitterly regretted the end but all mine welcomed it. Our parties before had been wild but now there was no restraint. At a parade of my small headquarters to announce the end, I shaved off my own moustache and then said to the Havildar Clerks, "All sahibs moustaches to be shaved off." We caught Tim and Stevens and their moustaches were soon off. They took it in good part. Many a sepoy must have told his children that in victory, the English celebrate by shaving off their moustaches.

The Engineers came flooding down the road to us, most of them bringing a bottle. At our mess that night we planned a grand Engineers' party to be held in Imphal. The Brigadier gave his approval and three days later all the officers and BORs in the plain were invited to a vast party. It started off with a point-to-point, in which I rode and fell off. The last point-to-point I had ridden in was in the Delhi Open Lightweight, which I would have won if I had been as good as my horse. I had got off last, passed all fourteen horses, lost a stirrup at a jump, circled while I recovered it, and then passed a further ten horses to finish fourth. My failure to win had been a real tragedy to my syce, who had backed me to win at 100–1 with all the money he had which was 20 rupees. To win over 2,000 rupees would have been equal to 4 years pay and I had let him down.

To return to the party; the Engineers had brought in rails and small tipper trucks and constructed 'the railway of victory'. We went round and round in the trucks and had to have a drink each time we passed 'Go'. Ted Goodbury was soon drunk and George, who always regarded himself as his warrant officer's keeper, pulled him almost drowning from a 4-foot-deep ditch. The party went on all night with food of all sorts, even fish and chips in newspaper, and singing and fights between some units. There was one thing missing: *girls*.

Shortly after this we had our first taste of the peacetime army. George Dorrington's workshop tended to get flooded when it rained, and he had erected a series of corrugated iron sheets to deflect the flash floods. His REME Colonel visited him.

"Dorrington, none of these slipshod wartime practices now. Get those sheets of corrugated iron whitewashed. We're a proper army now."

George still remembers the order with amazement.

The end of the Japanese war left us in the most extraordinary vacuum. Never before can a war have ended so unexpectedly. We had over two million men of the Indian Army under arms and now the purpose for which they had been trained had vanished.

What could we do with them? Two million men cannot just be disbanded and sent home. We continued therefore as an army but the mainspring of our existence was broken; the motive had gone. There seemed no purpose in anything, no reason for efficiency and now men began to scheme and plan for their own futures.

Just before the atom bombs were dropped plans were going ahead for the invasion of Singapore. The attack was planned in two waves: Zipper 1 and Zipper 2. We were part of the second wave which was due to go in on the third day of the action. As everything had already gone so far forward nothing was cancelled, possibly because there was some doubt as to whether or not the Japanese Singapore Command would go on fighting independently.

My company was ordered to move down to Calcutta which we did with ease. On arrival I gave away one of our two jeeps to a civilian tea planter from Darjeeling. He promised to give it a good home. The other jeep and our sailing boat we took with us. In the port we had to load the lorries on to ships which I think were called 'landing ship tanks' and were just like small cross-channel ferries. The loading in the docks of Calcutta went off quite happily until suddenly an unexpected problem arose. A rumour started among the higher caste Hindus that they would all lose caste when they crossed the sea. To our help came our faithful Brahmin, Paranjpe, who as long as he got a plentiful supply of drink could be relied on to do his best for us. Perhaps I am slandering him about the drink. He did have an intense loyalty to the British Raj and to the King Emperor. Paranjpe soon put all their minds at rest by assuring them that there was a ceremony which, on their return, would fully re-establish their caste.

We had a gentle journey down the Sunderbunds, that strange swampy delta area full of thick jungle and one of the main habitats of the tiger. As we came to the lifting of the waves near the mouth of the river, trouble began. The men were all asleep in cabins with bunks and were well accommodated. They began to feel seasick and the rumour swept through the whole Company that they had been poisoned by the food. If one had never heard of seasickness, one would put it down to something one had eaten.

By courtesy of the ship's officers we were quartered in their ward room. With a six-day journey in front of us we had relaxed and it took me a little time to realise that the men did not know what was wrong with them. Once we understood the problem the officers, with difficulty, restored confidence. Even so, it was like the worst days of our malaria collapse with all the men ill at the same time. A sick Madrassi makes the most of it and they appeared to be in the last stages of illness.

After three days, to their surprise the men began to recover. The journey then went very pleasantly. The gin was a great change from the eternal rum, and the ship had books I had not read before. By the time we came close to Singapore most of the men were fully fit again and we got ready for disembarkation in style.

It was so clear to everybody on shore that all resistance had ceased that nobody bothered to tell the convoy, and when we landed from the bows onto the slipway we headed out in full order ready for trouble. I was standing watching the lorries flow by and thinking how well the men now handled them when up rushed a young staff captain.

"Are you OC 309 Company?" he asked.

"Yes," I replied.

"Thank goodness I have found you," he said. "I have a special message from the Corps Commander." I jumped to the conclusion that there was serious trouble and that our lorries would be needed at once to help with the crisis. The staff officer continued.

"The cast of *Blithe Spirit* has flown in from London specially and they are opening at the theatre in four hours time. It is the first night and they have made a tremendous effort. So many units have not yet arrived we have only a half full theatre. The Corps Commander has instructed me to say that all your officers should attend the theatre this evening. Here are the tickets."

That was my first order on arriving in Singapore and it could not have been more welcome. *Blithe Spirit* was beautifully acted but those VCOs I took were quite bewildered; it was nothing like Shakespeare.

My orders were for the company to move to the Bukit Tima Golf Course. This was the premier golf course on the island and we were allocated the clubhouse for our officers' mess and living quarters; the men had comfortable accommodation nearby — luxury indeed. Shortly afterwards the secretary to the golf club, who had been a prisoner in Changi Jail, came to see me.

"Someone is riding over the fairways," he said. "Could you please stop them."

Next day I went out and, seeing two well-groomed horses, I went up to the Sikh Havildar in charge.

"When your Sahib comes, Havildar, please tell him to report to me at my office in the clubhouse."

"Yes, sahib," said the Havildar coming to attention. "When Lord Mountbatten sahib arrives, I will tell him to report to you at once."

"On second thoughts, Havildar," I said, "I will change my order. Please do not instruct the Admiral sahib to report to me."

"I will obey your new order, sahib," said the Havildar with a grin.

When we took over control of the city, we had re-established our old currency. The Japanese occupation currency had in one day become valueless. Their treasury had been a square room about 12 feet × 12 feet with no windows and in it were piles and piles of paper money. I was handed 1 million dollars, and I have it still — valueless and rather ugly. It brought home to me how dangerous paper money is; nothing holds it up in value but confidence and when that is gone, nothing remains but paper. Our troops were also issued with Japanese French letters about which they complained vigorously as being the wrong shape.

Boats of any sort were in very short supply on the island as the Japanese had destroyed most of them to prevent escapes. We sailed ours once or twice and then it was stolen. Perhaps it was just as well as sharks frequently travel from the Indian Ocean to the South China Sea and take a short cut round the bottom of Singapore Island; evidently they use regular pathways.

In my office early in December I opened a personal letter which was covered with postmarks. It was from the British Embassy in Denmark, dated May 1940 and invited me to stay. I read and reread the letter. It was from the Ambassador's daughter, posted the day before the German invasion. The envelope was covered with stamps from the Embassy, the German occupation forces, German post offices, British Army post offices, British and Singapore post offices, etc. It had been carefully held all those years by the Germans and, on their defeat, had been handed over with the Embassy post to the British Army. It was ridiculous of me, but I threw away the letter and the envelope. It would now not only be valuable but very interesting.

A large number of Dutch civilians, formerly Japanese prisoners, had been evacuated to Singapore and one of my new officers, Gordon Sheldon, made contact with a small group of girls. We took them out but when we called for them we noticed one pretty sixteen-year-old who was not allowed to come with us; she watched sadly as we left with the others. George Dorrington asked me to see what I could do about her. She and he had been exchanging glances. I called to see her father, who said:

"I did not bring my daughter safely through four years of a Japanese prison camp, Major Atkins, without her being once molested, to have her lose her virginity to a British Officer."

I was taken aback, particularly as all of us were really ridiculously innocent by present-day standards. I assured him that George was reliable and that I would make it my personal charge to see that his daughter was back safely from Raffles Hotel before midnight. Everything went well and we returned her on time from her first party ever. We soon got ourselves a reliable reputation among the Dutch families and their girls were allowed to come out with us regularly for parties and for dinner.

At one of these dinner parties, served in some style in the clubhouse, the duty VCO sent in an urgent message that he must see me at once. I went out.

"C Platoon," he said, "has mutinied. They have refused to attend roll call and the VCO (I forget his name) has run away and hidden."

C Platoon was the only one not under the command of a King's Officer but I had been so busy enjoying myself that I had not paid enough attention to what was happening in the Company. I should have taken note of some of the hints my Subahdar Adjutant had given me but the army had lost its importance in my eyes. I must by that time have been very sure of myself, for instead of going down or sending an officer, I gave a verbal message to the duty VCO, saying:

"Don't be such bloody fools. If there is any more disobeying of orders there will be much trouble. I order you now go straight to bed. I will hold a Platoon Durbar tomorrow morning at first parade."

The VCO went off, gave them the message, and they all went to bed. A situation which might easily have developed into quite a storm with a few court martials was all over in a few minutes. When I saw the platoon the following morning, I found their dissatisfaction was over the way the extra food allowance was being spent. The other platoons were getting considerably better food than C Platoon because their VCO, a Punjabi, was not using the money sensibly but was buying northern-type food.

I was now due to go home and was instructed to hand over to Tim Eaton who was to be promoted Major. He was due to follow me home in two to three months. Having heard that there were no spirits available in England and that the only luggage we could take on board was what each man could carry, he was planning to have two strengthened suitcases made; he then intended to fill them up with bottles of rum and gin, and totter on board with all he could carry.

My last two weeks were riotously happy. All my officers and VCOs went out of their way to give me a tremendous send-off. The Dutch girls had emerged like butterflies from the chrysalis of four years of harsh Japanese prison discipline. They blossomed day by day, their very shape changing as they put on curves to arms, cheeks and breasts which a few weeks before had been only skin and bone. I think they all genuinely and innocently loved us all as individuals and as a group. They were as tireless as puppies as they explored the new world which opened around them day by day.

George was Mess Secretary and he spared no effort. Christmas lunch had turkey, a Christmas pudding flaming with brandy, a bottle of port and real coffee. George even found an imitation Christmas tree which had been kept hidden by a trader for the four years of occupation. The mess was ablaze with flowers set amongst palm leaves.

On Boxing Day in the magnificent dining room we gave a full dinner for the families of the Dutch girls. Twenty-two sat down at the polished table and we formally toasted Queen Wilhelmena of The Netherlands before we toasted the King. The candlelight played on the faces of parents grown pinched and grey in prison and the miracle of their daughters blossoming into beauty.

I arranged a farewell nautch party for the men and engaged some Javanese dancers. I could hardly stand up for the weight of the garlands round my neck and here I made my main leaving speech. It is easy to speak in a simple language; sentiment does not sound absurd.

"For four years we have worked together. We started badly, they laughed at this Madrasi Company, this bad company, and then we became the best company, the absolutely top company of all the Transport Companies, this Madrasi Company. My heart goes well to all your hearts and I will not forget you all my life. I will always remember our Madrasi Company, which we made together, you and I."

Then there were parties to say goodbye to the VCOs and NCOs, and finally the girls and my officers gave me a farewell party at the Tanglin Club. The girls had stitched their names on a white silk scarf and the officers gave me a silver cigarette box.

They all came to see me off on the *Winchester Castle*, already repainted in its own colours. As soon as I sailed I was brought down to earth with a bump. Majors were so numerous we had to queue for everything — there were more of us because the junior ranks had not yet reached their demobilisation group.

I arrived back in England to stay with my father. As my mother had died during the war, the house seemed very large and lonely. I had virtually no clothes except my sepoy's uniform but the army turned up trumps. Everyone else was very scornful of the issue of civilian clothes which were doled out to all returning soldiers at Olympia. My brother-in-law gave me a second lot of demobilisation tickets and I went up and found there a flannel pin-stripe suit made by Gieves and a tweed one made by Austin Reed; they were really very good. I also emerged with two hats, good shoes, shirts and underwear. These clothes would have taken four years' supply of clothing coupons. Every tailor in England had made the suits and their names were somewhere to be found if one took the trouble. It was a magnificent effort.

One other thing — no officer on demobilisation received a large gratuity. This is a myth which springs from the generous gratuities of the First World War. One just got the leave pay due to one plus in my case £145. A year or so passed and a letter came from the Queen authorising me to use the title Major for the rest of my life, but as I am not a regular I do not of course use it. Twenty more years passed and I received the Territorial Medal (TM) not the Territorial Decoration (TD) as I had been in the ranks in September 1939.

To end on a true but depressing note; while still emaciated and bright yellow — at least I had stopped smelling like a rat — I worked too hard for my chartered accountant's examination. I passed it but was so exhausted mentally I was unable to work again for well over a year. Without realising it I had become a minor war casualty. I remarked on this the other day to my wife — a doctor.

"Of course you were a war casualty," she said. "I always thought of you as such." Oh dear, and I never claimed a pension. Perhaps it's not too late.

* * * * *

APPENDIX I
(see page 116)

In April 1943 all British officers attached to the Indian Army, as I then was, had been asked to volunteer for transfer to the Indian Army. I applied, had had no reply, and had forgotten the matter. In November 1944 GHQ changed the rules for leave to England and at the same time they transferred to the Indian Army proper all officers who had volunteered twenty months before. This meant that I, as a volunteer, would rank for leave after eight years' service in India, while all my officers were due for one month's leave after the incredibly short period of 18 months' service in India. It was really a very dirty trick, presumably carried out by some bureaucratic-minded staff officer in Delhi. There is much in the Army maxim 'Never volunteer'. I wrote some letters on the position and the one which follows was published by the Editor of SEAC, Frank Owen. He had been promoted from 2nd Lieutenant to Brigadier by Mountbatten on starting the newspaper for the South East Asia Command (SEAC). This paper was published daily and was delivered free to every unit on the Burma front.

Wednesday, 17th January 1945   SEAC Newspaper

Letter from
Major D.R. Atkins, GPT Coy, S.E.A.C.

The position of the officer recruited in England who 'volunteered' for the Indian Army, before conditions of repatriation and demobilisation were published, is as follows:
1. He cannot be repatriated on long service grounds.
2. He cannot be repatriated on compassionate grounds.
3. For leave he ranks below all officers of the Indian Army recruited in India. These officers count their civilian service during and

before the war as service overseas. There is therefore a very long list for leave, and under an order published in December only those with eight years service overseas are permitted to apply.
4. If he has service of over 2½ years and under 6 years he may get 28 days leave under the new scheme.
5. He is demobilised under the Indian Government Scheme. This will begin to operate only after the end of the Japanese war. Thus a Class 20 ECO of the Indian Army may be demobilised many months or years after a Class 20 ECO of the British Army. (ECO means Emergency Commissioned Officer.)
6. If wounded three times he does not get repatriation.

Compare his position with the British Service officer attached to the Indian Army, whose position is:

1. He has the right to repatriation before 5 years service overseas. The period now is just over 4 years.
2. He may be repatriated at any time on compassionate grounds.
3. If he does not wish to be repatriated he has a right to two months leave after 4 years service overseas.
4. He may get 28 days home leave at any time before 2½ years overseas service.
5. He is demobilised under the British Scheme long before the man of the same age and service of the Indian Army.
6. If wounded three times he is repatriated.
7. He gets the same rate of pay as the Officers of the Indian Army.

People in Britain are misled by the term British Service Personnel of the Indian Army, otherwise they would not tolerate the treatment of the British Personnel (not British Service) of the Indian Army who volunteered.

APPENDIX II
by George Dorrington

When I arrived at 309 GPT Company, I was fresh out from England. Unlike many REME officers who were attached to Transport Companies, I was at once absorbed in the friendliest manner into the officers' mess. The fact that I thought everyone extraordinary was by the way; David regarded me as an asset and so from the first I set out to help. This was the strength of the Company — we were all out to help each other.

When I took my first workshop parade I was bewildered by the sameness of the faces and the lack of expression in them. This was my own blindness, and in a short time they all sprang into focus as individuals. How different they were! I had Madrassis and Mahrattas, Bengalis and Pathans, Hindus and Mohammedans — and eight different languages. They all had one thing in common: they wanted us to understand them.

In a British unit there are normally some bloody-minded men as NCOs; not so in my platoon. I had a British Warrant Officer junior in rank to my Punjabi VCO, a Madrassi Havildar Clerk, and a Brahmin in my stores. The British Warrant Officer taught me about lorries, the Punjabi taught me Urdu, the Clerk taught me army procedure, and overall all the Company had that indefinable thing — *esprit de corps* — the pride in itself without which nothing runs well. That is what made my time with 309 so enjoyable.

Bishops Stortford
July 1988

APPENDIX III

After this book was ready for printing, while on holiday in Vienna, I met John Constable.

At the time of the 'flap', he was a major on the staff at Dimapur. On a morning late in March, probably the 27th, Constable was instructed to meet 161 Brigade of 5 Division which was flying in.

It was only just light when he reached the airstrip, which had been carved out of thick jungle. There was no one there except two RAF NCOs. Constable asked if everything was ready.

"The strip is closed today, waterlogged. Nothing can come in Sir."

"The Brigade is on its way, it's almost here. Better check with your Headquarters."

The NCO came back badly shaken.

"You're quite right Sir, but I'll fire a red Verey light to stop them. There's two inches of water over the pierced steel planks." These were the only foundation and were laid direct on the soft mud.

Constable, who was a sapper, walked across the strip. He thought the planks might just hold. He knew the Japanese were near.

"I instruct you to accept the planes," he said.

"Not likely, it's impossible to land."

"Hand me the Verey lights and pistol and I'll do it myself."

"Look here Sir, I'm RAF and you're Army. I'm not handing over to you."

"This is an order," said Constable, "and you will obey it."

The RAF NCO consulted his junior.

"OK, but it's all your responsibility and nothing to do with me."

John took the pistol and the cartridges from him. Never had he felt so nervous. If he let the planes land they might all crash. If he did not, Dimapur with its vast stores and depots, might fall to the Japanese.

The first plane arrived, circled, and he fired a green Verey light. The plane landed and disappeared from sight in spray 30 feet high. For several seconds nothing happened and then its nose emerged. He fired another Verey light and the next plane started its descent.

That is how 161 Brigade landed in time to stop the Japanese reaching Dimapur.

The first Brigade of 2 Division did not reach Dimapur until 2nd April.

POSTSCRIPT

On page 115 I mention the loss of all my clothes. In France in 1940, when the Germans struck, my boots were at the cobblers.

The British army moved up into Belgium and after a fortnight I was given permission to go back and fetch my boots. I drove back through the French sector to the village of Fouquière which I found in turmoil and despair. From the war memorial steps I made a speech in my schoolboy French: "Maintenant nous departons mais nous retournerons." My boots were not ready.

I drove north out of the square and turned left at the next crossroads. Ten minutes later German tanks came into the village down the same road.

When I returned after the war, Capitain and Madame Blanvarlet told me they had been certain I had been captured or killed. As the British prisoners of war streamed down the main road the boots were hurriedly repaired and the Blanvarlets, with their daughters Solange and Marie-Lou, took it in turns for five days to stand, boots in hand, watching for me. For the girls in particular it was a brave thing to do.